Jagdstaffel 2
'Boelcke'

OSPREY
PUBLISHING

Jagdstaffel 2
'Boelcke'

Greg VanWyngarden
Series editor Tony Holmes

Front Cover
The skies were fairly clear over Flanders on 9 March 1918 when 21-year-old Vfw Paul Bäumer went looking for trouble. Bäumer was one of the most accomplished pilots in the prestigious *Jasta* 'Boelcke', with 18 victories already to his name. The superbly manoeuvrable Fokker Dr I 204/17 he was piloting was perfectly suited to Bäumer's flying skill and preferred tactics. He penned the following report upon returning to base upon the completion of his morning patrol;

'Location and time – one kilometre north of Zonnebeke at 1110 hrs. I was flying with four other men from the *Staffel* to the Wytschaete Bend when we saw three single-seater flights of seven aircraft each flying in formation to our front. We attacked the lower flight at a height of 2000 metres over Becelaere. First I had a banking fight with a Sopwith that I had to break off from again. Then I followed three Sopwith single-seaters from the same flight which were flying together. At a height of 1500 metres, I attacked one of these, whereupon he flew towards me. After a short banking fight, I, from close range, caused the Sopwith to crash. The Sopwith reared up and then dived down vertically. I followed the falling opponent and saw him run vertically into the ground north of the Zonnebeke-Frezenberg road. The aircraft was completey smashed up (destroyed).'

It appears that *Jasta* 'Boelcke' was in combat with Sopwith Camels from No 65 Sqn that morning. Capt G M Cox reported;

'The formation was attacked by several Fokker triplanes. I saw one of them get on the tail of one of our machines. I got into good position and put in a burst of about 50 rounds into him at about 1500 ft, when one of his planes folded up.'

Bäumer was credited with his 20th victory on this day and *Jasta* 'Boelcke' suffered no losses. It appears that both sides may have made over-optimistic claims – not an unusual occurrence in the hotly contested skies over Ypres. Nonetheless, Bäumer would go on to achieve 43 victories, and survive the war as the top-scoring pilot of *Jasta* 'Boelcke' (*Cover artwork by Mark Postlethwaite*)

First published in Great Britain in 2007 by Osprey Publishing
Midland House, West Way, Botley, Oxford, OX2 0PH
443 Park Avenue South, New York, NY, 10016, USA
E-mail; info@ospreypublishing.com

ISBN 10: 1 84603 203 2
ISBN 13: 978 1 84603 203 5

Edited by Tony Holmes
Page design by Mark Holt
Cover Artwork by Mark Postlethwaite
Aircraft Profiles by Harry Dempsey
Index by Alan Thatcher

Printed in China

07 08 09 10 11   10 9 8 7 6 5 4 3 2 1

For a catalogue of all books published by Osprey please contact:
NORTH AMERICA
Osprey Direct, C/o Random House Distribution Center,
400 Hahn Road, Westminster, MD 21157
E-mail:info@ospreydirect.com

ALL OTHER REGIONS
Osprey Direct UK, PO Box 140 Wellingborough, Northants, NN8 2FA, UK
E-mail: info@ospreydirect.co.uk
www.ospreypublishing.com

CONTENTS

DEBUT OVER THE SOMME

It is likely that everyone with an interest in aviation history has heard of Rittmeister Manfred *Freiherr* von Richthofen – known as the 'Red Baron', and the top-scoring fighter ace of World War 1 with 80 victories. Almost as famous is *Jagdstaffel* 11, the fighter squadron he commanded, usually abbreviated as *Jasta* 11. Von Richthofen would not have become as successful without the training he received while serving under the man he regarded as his mentor and the Father of German Fighter Aviation – Hptm Oswald Boelcke. Von Richthofen began his career as a fighter pilot in Boelcke's *Jasta* 2, and it was under Boelcke's careful and demanding tutelage that he honed his skills.

After Boelcke's death, the unit that he had commanded was officially re-named *Jasta* 'Boelcke' in his honour. The *Staffel* continued to serve through frustrating periods of failure and mediocrity as well as great success, and finished the conflict with a record of accomplishment and prestige second to none.

The story of *Jasta* 2 is intertwined with that of its first commander. On 19 May 1891, Oswald Boelcke was born in Giebichenstein, a suburb of Halle an der Saale in Prussia. He was the fourth son of a professor who was rector at the German Lutheran school at the time Oswald was born. When the boy was four the family moved to Dessau, capital city of the duchy of Anhalt. Boelcke contracted whooping cough as a youth, but built up his strength and stamina through strenuous participation in such sports as rowing, swimming and gymnastics. Nonetheless, he suffered from asthma for the rest of his life. Boelcke's interest in mechanics influenced his entrance as a fahnenjunker, or officer cadet, in *Telegraphen-Bataillon* Nr 3 in Koblenz during March 1911.

By June 1914, as war loomed on the horizon, Oswald had followed his elder brother Wilhelm into the aviation service and started his pilot training. Wilhelm duly became an observer in two-seater reconnaissance formation *Feldflieger Abteilung* (F Fl Abt) 13 after the war broke out. He managed to have Oswald sent to his unit, and the two formed a highly successful team. In April 1915 Ltn Oswald Boelcke was posted to the newly formed F Fl Abt 62, along with a Saxon flier named Max Immelmann. The unit was based at Pont Faverger, near Douai in France.

On 4 July 1915, Boelcke was piloting an Albatros C I two-seater equipped with a machine gun for his observer, Ltn von Wühlisch, when the pair attacked a French Morane two-seater. Boelcke carefully positioned his aircraft so as to give von Wühlisch the best possible chance of shooting their opponent down. Struck by a series of well aimed bursts, the Morane crashed behind German lines. As a direct result of this engagement, Boelcke was subsequently given a better aircraft to fly in combat.

The Master, Hptm Oswald Boelcke. Besides being a superb fighter pilot, Boelcke was an excellent instructor who was dedicated to passing on to his pilots the tactics he had developed through his own experiences. During the Great War, Boelcke was revered by both the *Fliegertruppe* and the German population, arguably even more than von Richthofen

Dutch aircraft designer Anthony Fokker had recently introduced his E I design, which held great promise for aggressive pilots like Boelcke. The Fokker E I was a monoplane with a revolutionary synchronised machine gun mounted to fire through the whirling propeller. Boelcke was soon flying his monoplane at every opportunity. Immelmann was also flying a Fokker, and it fell to him to score the first Eindecker victory for F Fl Abt 62 on 1 August 1915 (see *Osprey Aircraft of the Aces 73 - Early German Aces of World War 1* for further details).

Both pilots had taken off to intercept British BE 2c two-seaters on a bombing raid, but Boelcke suffered a jammed gun while Immelmann shot down one of the Royal Flying Corps (RFC) aircraft. Boelcke was eager to achieve his own victory in a Fokker, and on 19 August he was credited with downing what was likely another BE 2c. The competition was on, and Immelmann and Boelcke continued knocking down Allied aircraft, reaping honours and national celebrity. Other Fokker pilots were starting to gain victories as well, and the succeeding period of Eindecker superiority is sometimes known as the 'Fokker Scourge'.

In September 1915, Boelcke was transferred to Metz on the Champagne Front. He was attached to a large formation called *Brieftauben-Abteilung Metz* (*BAM*). Literally, this meant 'Carrier Pigeon Section', which was a cover name for an offensive unit with the strength of about four *Flieger Abteilungen.* This was the second such formation, the first being *Brieftauben-Abteilung Ostende* (*BAO*). Boelcke's growing command of fighter tactics was evident on 25 September when he shot down a French bomber from a formation attacking Metz.

A few days later he was travelling by train to a new area of operations when his fame brought recognition by a 23-year-old Silesian leutnant. The young uhlan (lancer) officer was named Manfred von Richthofen, then a completely unknown pilot of the *BAO*. Clearly in awe of the great Boelcke, von Richthofen approached him and managed to ask, 'Tell me, honestly, how do you do it?' Impressed by the stranger's eagerness, Boelcke kindly discussed his aerial combat techniques with him and filed his name away in his memory.

Boelcke and Immelmann's victory count continued to increase, along with their decorations. After Boelcke's sixth victory on 30 October, he became the first airman to earn the Knight's Cross of the House of Hohenzollern with Swords. Immelmann was also soon decorated with the 'Hohenzollern'. After each of the pair gained their eighth success, they were surprised to learn that they would be presented with the *Orden Pour le Mérite*, the high Prussian award popularly known as the 'Blue Max'.

KEKs

By the end of 1915, plans were underway for the grouping of Eindeckers into separate, temporary detachments based at one aerodrome. Such a formation was generally called a *Kampfeinsitzer-Kommando* or *KEK*. These units were but one of several changes organised by the *Chef des Feldflugwesens* (or *Feldflugchef*, the Chief of Field Aviation), Maj Hermann von der Lieth-Thomsen.

Three such temporary units would be part of the aerial forces gathered on the German 5. *Armee* Front for the assault on Verdun that began on 21 February 1916. Boelcke was assigned to the *KEK* based at Jametz, but he obtained permission to establish a small detachment of Fokkers at the forward airfield at Sivry in early March. Here, he initiated a groundbreaking system in which his base was connected to a forward observation post by telephone. His Sivry *Kommando* could now be informed when the arrival of French aeroplanes was imminent, allowing he or his pilots to take off in plenty of time to intercept them. As always, Boelcke was in the lead in the development of fighter tactics, and he received credit for a Voisin bomber on 13 March as his 11th victory.

The days of the 'Fokker Scourge' were fast drawing to a close, however. The conflict over Verdun saw the introduction of the excellent Nieuport 11 – a single-seat fighter with a Lewis gun mounted on the top wing. The Nieuports clearly had the upper hand over the Fokkers when it came to manoeuvrability, speed and climb (see *Osprey Aircraft of the Aces 33 - Nieuport Aces of World War 1* for further details). Better British aeroplanes were also making their appearance. In February 1916, the RFC's No 24 Sqn arrived in France equipped with the new DH 2 single-seat 'pusher' fighter. The unit was aggressively led by Maj Lanoe Hawker VC DSO, the first British ace and a legendary pioneer of fighter tactics and technology.

Early 1916 also saw the first use of the well-armed FE 2b two-seater pusher. Indeed, it was during an attack on FE 2bs from No 25 Sqn on 18 June that Max Immelmann fell. German airmen believed that Immelmann was the victim of a malfunction of his gun synchronisation gear. Whatever the cause, the great hero was dead, and his fate was another signal of the end of the Eindecker era.

June 1916 also ushered in a massive build-up of Allied aerial forces in support of the Somme Offensive, planned for 1 July, against the German 2. *Armee*. Some 167 British aeroplanes assembled on the Somme front, and the French contributed even more aircraft. With much of the German Air Service concentrated at Verdun, aerial units of the 2. *Armee* began the Somme battle facing a three-to-one Allied superiority in aircraft.

The Germans knew something was brewing on the Somme front, and Hptm Oswald Boelcke was eager to be part of the aerial response to it. When he returned to Sivry after attending Immelmann's funeral, he discovered a telegram ordering him to report to the *Feldflugchef*. He joyfully anticipated being transferred to the Somme, but instead received a crushing disappointment. He wrote to his parents;

'The *Chef* made a long speech, the purport of which was that I was to sit in a glass case in Charleville – I was not to fly at all for the present because my "nerves" must be rested, but I could organise a Fokker *Staffel* in Charleville. Well, you can just imagine my rage!'

The High Command did not wish to risk the loss of another great aerial hero so soon after Immelmann's death, so Boelcke was grounded by imperial order. He soon took the opportunity to go on an official mission to Turkey and the Eastern Front as an alternative to the proposed desk job. Before he left, Boelcke spent several days meeting with the *Feldflugchef* and his staff. The great ace outlined his principles for aerial combat, the famous 'Dicta Boelcke' that remained the basic guidelines for German fighter pilots throughout the war. Furthermore, he emphasised that new and permanent formations of single-seaters were necessary, and that it was also essential to train all the pilots of such a unit to fly with strict formation discipline and 'thus organise aerial warfare'. In this way Boelcke planted the seed which would eventually bear fruit in the creation of the first *Jagdstaffeln* by von der Lieth-Thomsen on 10 August 1916.

With an overwhelming superiority in both numbers and quality of aircraft, the Allies quickly seized control of the skies over the Somme battlefront. DH 2s and Nieuports forced the German fighters away from the front, allowing their own reconnaissance and bombing machines to roam into the airspace beyond the German lines almost undisturbed. As the situation above the Somme grew ever more desperate, Boelcke was still on his mandatory holiday tour of the East. He had travelled from Turkey to Macedonia, and on to Bulgaria. Then he headed to Kovel, in Ukraine, in order to visit his brother. Wilhelm was now commanding *Kampfstaffel* 10, one of component units of *Kagohl* II.

The *Kagohl* was a large offensive formation consisting of six *Kasta*, each equipped with six armed two-seaters. On 11 August 1916, a momentous telegram from the *Feldflugchef* caught up with Oswald Boelcke;

'Return to Western Front as quickly as possible to organise and lead *Jagdstaffel* 2 on the Somme front.'

Now Boelcke had the choice assignment he hungered for. He used some of the time he had left with his brother to discuss the merits of various pilots they knew for inclusion in his new unit. Wilhelm apparently recommended at least two of the pilots in *Kagohl* II, and both were very astute choices. One was the cavalryman Manfred von Richthofen, then a pilot with *Kasta* 8. 'Suddenly in the morning there was a knock on the door and before me stood the great man with the *Pour le Mérite*,' recounted von Richthofen. 'I really did not know what he expected of me. To be sure, I knew him, but it did not occur to me that he had sought me out to invite me to become a pupil of his. I could have hugged him when he asked whether I wanted to go to the Somme with him.'

In mid-August 1916, Boelcke visited his brother Wilhelm, the commander of *Kasta* 10 of *Kagohl* II, based at Kovel on the Eastern Front. Boelcke asked the *Kagohl* pilots Erwin Böhme and Manfred von Richthofen to join the new *Jagdstaffel* he would be forming in the west. Böhme is seen in the front cockpit of Albatros C III 766/16 that he flew at *Kasta* 10, with his observer Ltn Lademacher. Böhme wrote that his C III had been decorated with a fierce dragon, which 'at least made a terrifying impression on the Russian peasants'. The insignia was quite different on each side of the C III, for on the port side it resembled some fantastic crocodilian creature (*N Franks*)

The other pilot selected by Boelcke seemed an unlikely choice. Born in Holzminden on 29 July 1879, Ltn d R Erwin Böhme was an 'old man' at 37, but a respected pilot in *Kasta* 10. Before the war he had spent six years working as an engineer in German East Africa, where he oversaw the construction of the Usambara cable railway. He had done his compulsory military service in the *Garde-Jäger-Bataillon* in Potsdam, and returned to that unit when the war broke out. Böhme managed a transfer to the Army Air Service, and after serving as a flight instructor he joined *Kasta* 10 in December 1915. He flew bombing missions in the Verdun offensive, and first met the great Boelcke when he visited Wilhelm on 5 March 1916.

In May Böhme was promoted to Leutnant der Reserve, and travelled east with the rest of *Kagohl* II in July. Perhaps because of his maturity and experience, Böhme would become Boelcke's closest personal friend. According to Böhme's letters, Boelcke also selected three others from *Kagohl* II, but their identities are unconfirmed.

Boelcke and the men he had chosen hurried westward by various routes. 27 August found the *Staffelführer* checking over the large airfield at Bertincourt, some 20 kilometres east of Cambrai in the 1. *Armee* sector. The aerodrome was large and well developed. It had already served as the base for several units, including *KEK* Bertincourt (*KEK* B), which provided the nucleus for nearby *Jasta* 1, commanded by Hptm Martin Zander. Boelcke selected four sturdy wooden hangar sheds on the southeast corner of the Velu woods, hidden by the foliage of the nearby trees. The first entry in the *Staffel* war diary begins on the 27th, and states; '*Jagdstaffel* 2 assembled under the leadership of Hptm Boelcke. Effectives – three officers (Ltn d Rs Hans von Arnim and Wolfgang Günther, in addition to Boelcke), 64 NCOs and men. Quarters – officers to be billeted in Bertincourt, men to live in huts. Machines – none to hand as yet. Activities – preparation of aerodrome.'

Von Arnim would never fly with *Jasta* 2, although he was technically on its rolls. He was still flying with his old unit Fl Abt (A) 207 when he was killed on the 28th by a No 60 Sqn Nieuport flown by RFC ace Capt Albert Ball. On the 29th, Hptm Zander helped Boelcke out by transferring some mechanics and 21-year-old Ltn Otto Höhne from his *Jasta* 1.

Also arriving was Ltn Winand Grafe from *KEK* B, and Ltn Ernst Diener from *Kagohl* 6. On 1 September Richthofen showed up, as well as Bavarian Offz Stv (acting officer) Max Müller and Ltn d R Hans Reimann. The 23-year-old Saxon Offz Stv Leopold Reimann (no relation to Hans) was also posted in after having scored the first victory for *Jasta* 1 on 24 August. He brought along an Albatros D I (probably 385/16) on 1 September. The same day two Fokker biplanes were ferried in from *Armee Flug Park* 1, with Boelcke taking over Fokker D III 352/16. He put it to good use the very next day, scoring the first victory for *Jasta* 2 – and his own 20th.

COUNTERING BRITISH RECONNAISSANCE FLIGHTS

In preparation for the third phase in the Battle of the Somme, the British were making increased reconnaissance patrols. One such BE 2c flight on 2 September was being escorted by two No 32 Sqn DH 2s (which the Germans erroneously and consistently called 'Vickers' fighters) when they ran into Boelcke, who later wrote;

Boelcke is seen in a typical pose on Bertincourt airfield with his Fokker D III 352/16 – the first fighter he flew with *Jasta* 2. He scored his 20th victory in this machine on 2 September 1916, which was also the first success for his new *Jagdstaffel*

'I saw flak bursts west of Bapaume. And there I found a BE biplane and three Vickers single-seaters. That meant an artillery spotting aircraft and its escort. I chose the BE first, but in the middle of my attack the other three disturbed me – so, I decided to retreat – whereupon one of the Vickers believed he could get me, and placed himself behind me.'

The 'Vickers' was DH 2 7895, flown by Capt R E Wilson of No 32 Sqn, who later penned this account;

'After I had fired several bursts at the German he turned and flew home. I followed him, and noticed he was luring me further and further into his territory, and after I had followed him for 15 miles he turned round and attacked, and with unbelievable speed climbed above me.

'He was flying a type of aircraft I had never seen before, and I had no idea of its speed and rate of climb. My machine gun jammed after I had fired a few rounds – and under those circumstances the only thing I could do was flee. I tried every trick to get away, but he was able to skilfully follow my every move, and stayed right behind me. He shot through all my control cables except two – and these were jammed! My coat was also holed in two places, and soaked in patrol. Naturally, I lost all control over my machine. When at about 50 ft above the ground I pulled the controls back and forth, and somehow at the last moment obtained enough control to make some sort of landing – during which the machine and my coat burst into flames. I found it was possible to jump out and throw my coat off – and was not burnt.'

Wilson was made a PoW, and the next day he met Boelcke. When introduced, Wilson said, 'If I had to be shot down, I'm pleased that it should have been by so good a man'. He was taken to Bertincourt for coffee and a tour of the aerodrome.

For the next two weeks Boelcke worked tirelessly, training his eager pupils and finding time to down six more aircraft. Every time he returned from a flight, his fledglings would gather round and ask if he had downed another Englishman for 'breakfast'. Boelcke would respond, 'Is my chin black?' Powder stains on his face indicated that his guns had been fired and another enemy had fallen. He hammered his fundamental rules for air combat – the 'Dicta Boelcke' – into his students. These rules were laconically expressed as –

'1. Seek advantage before attacking. If possible, keep the sun at your back.

'2. Having begun an attack, always follow through.

'3. Only fire at short range, and only when your opponent is positively in your sights.

'4. Never lose sight of your opponent, and do not be fooled by his tricks.

'5. In every attack it is important to approach your opponent from behind.

'6. If your opponent attacks from above, do not try to evade but fly to meet him.

'7. When over enemy territory, never forget your path home.

'8. For the *Staffel* – attack on principle in flights of four or six. When single combat ensues, take care that many do not go for one opponent.'

Boelcke proved the effectiveness of his methods by flaming an FE 2b on 8 September and burning a No 24 Sqn DH 2 the next day. On the 10th Ltn d R Herwarth Phillips was transferred in from *KEK* Vaux. The next day Böhme wrote that he had been allowed to use a 'refurbished' Halberstadt, giving the unit a total of four aircraft. The *Staffelführer* began taking his charges on small group sorties. On 14 September Boelcke, Böhme and von Richthofen attacked some Sopwith two-seaters of No 70 Sqn. Boelcke sent one down minus its top wing and his two comrades scrapped with the others, gaining valuable experience.

On the 14th the hauptmann forced down another DH 2 from No 24 Sqn intact – it was brought to *Jasta* 2 so Boelcke could use it 'as a means of instruction' for his eager pilots. A brace of Sopwiths from the luckless No 70 Sqn fell to the consistently deadly *Jasta* commander the very next day.

The arrival of six new Albatros fighters (five D Is and one D II) at *Jasta* 2 on 16 September 1916 caused a great deal of excitement. The D I at left is probably 384/16, one of the prototype aircraft that had the expansion tank placed in front of the engine. Most other D Is had the standard triangular expansion tank fitted over the engine. Boelcke's Fokker D III 352/16 is still on hand at right (*A E Ferko*)

On 16 September *Armee Flug Park* 1 telephoned Boelcke with the exciting news that six new Albatros fighters had arrived for his *Jasta*. These consisted of five D Is, and the first D II (386/16), which became Boelcke's personal machine. There was great enthusiasm for the powerful new aeroplanes as Böhme explained to his future fiancée, Annamarie Brüning;

'Our new machines likewise border on marvellous. They are far improved over the single-seaters we flew at Verdun. Their climb rate and manoeuvrability are astonishing – it is as if they were living, feeling beings that understand what their master wishes. With them, one can dare and achieve everything.'

The evening of that same Saturday, Ltn Höhne downed a No 11 Sqn 'Fee' for the first *Staffel* victory achieved by a pilot other than Boelcke.

The career of *Jasta* 2 as a cohesive fighting unit can really be dated from 17 September 1916. Boelcke wrote home that morning;

'The *Staffel* is not quite up to strength yet, as I am still without about half of our machines. But yesterday at least six arrived, so that I shall be able to take off with my *Staffel* for the first time today.'

At 0745 hrs that morning Böhme used his D I to despatch another Sopwith two-seater from the beleaguered No 70 Sqn for his first victory. The sleek Albatros fighters then returned to Bertincourt, where they were prepared for another sortie as more RFC aircraft had been sighted crossing the lines. BEs from No 12 Sqn were on their way to bomb Marcoing railway station, escorted by six FE 2bs from No 11 Sqn.

At Bertincourt the grumble of Mercedes engines filled the air as Boelcke led four of his 'pups' off in pursuit. *Jasta* 2 knifed into the

Hptm Boelcke is assisted with his scarf as he prepares for flight in his Albatros D II 386/16 at Lagnicourt airfield. This was one of the first D IIs to arrive at the front

Ltn d R Otto Höhne was credited with the first victory scored by a *Jasta* 2 pilot other than Boelcke when he downed an FE 2b on the evening of 16 September, possibly while in one of the newly-arrived Albatros D I fighters. Here is a later photograph of Höhne taking off in his D I 390/16. In common with many other aircraft in the unit, his machine has been marked with an abbreviation of his name, in this case *Hö* painted on both sides of the fuselage (*P M Grosz*)

formation of some 14 aeroplanes west of Marcoing just as the BEs dropped their bombs. Von Richthofen selected FE 2b 7018 and closed to within ten metres of his quarry as he fired, nearly ramming it in his excitement. His shots killed the observer and mortally wounded the pilot, who nonetheless managed to bring the crippled pusher down to a dead stick landing near Villers Plouich. Von Richthofen landed nearby to observe as the crew was pulled from his first confirmed victory – 79 more would follow.

At almost the same time, Hans Reimann brought down another aircraft south of Trescault. Boelcke himself selected the FE 2b flown by Flight Commander Capt D B Gray and Lt L Helder;

'I engaged the leader's machine, which I recognised by its streamers, and forced it down. My opponent landed at Equancourt and promptly set fire to his machine. The occupants were taken prisoner – one of them was slightly wounded. The pilot had to land because I shot his engine to pieces. So that was No 27.'

Boelcke had ample reason to be pleased with his fledglings. Böhme wrote;

'On Sunday afternoon, our as-yet-incomplete fighter squadron had a small party to celebrate its inauguration and the day's first successes. At our celebration, Boelcke pinned on me the Iron Cross First Class, which had just arrived.'

On the 16th Ltn Hellmuth von Zastrow was posted in as OzbV (Officer for Special Duties, or adjutant) to assist Boelcke with the paperwork required in a new unit.

Boelcke brought his own tally to 28 on 19 September with a Morane monoplane from No 60 Sqn. 'Six of us rattled into a squadron of eight or ten FE biplanes and several Moranes', he recounted. 'The fat *Gitterschwänze* (lattice-tails, slang for pushers) were below, with the Moranes above as cover. I engaged one of the latter and pranced about the air with him – he escaped me for a moment, but I got to grips with him again west of Bapaume – one of my guns jammed, but the other shot all the better. I shot up the monoplane from close range until he broke up in flames and fell in fragments into the woods near Grévillers'.

The RFC struck back on 19 September, as single-seat BE 12s of Nos 19 and 21 Sqn bombed the Velu/Bertincourt airfield. All the RFC airmen reported hot fighting. At day's end Höhne and both Reimanns had each destroyed one BE 12. However the Boelcke *Staffel* suffered its first combat casualty when Ltn Winand Grafe was killed, reportedly on his fourth flight of the day. No 19 Sqn's 2Lt V R Stewart was attacked by a rotary engined biplane (possibly Grafe in a Fokker D III) which Stewart then shot down in flames. No 60 Sqn's Capt Albert Ball also attacked a Fokker biplane on this date and has been credited by some with Grafe's demise. It was a sobering day for Boelcke's pilots.

The area around Bertincourt was also receiving attention from British artillery, and on the night of 22/23 September the *Staffel* transferred some nine kilometres north to Lagnicourt. The move was accomplished under the leadership of Oblt Günther Viehweger because Boelcke was incapacitated by the return of his asthma. The illness was so severe that Boelcke's orderly Fischer was hardly able to transport him to the new aerodrome – the *Staffelführer* stubbornly refused to go to hospital, but did not resume flying until the 27th.

Ltn d R Wolfgang Günther was a charter member of *Jasta* 2. Here he appears ready for flight in front of his Albatros D I 426/16, which had the fuselage camouflaged in a dark colour (or colours) with a light blue underside

Nonetheless, Boelcke's pilots took off from the new site on the 23rd, and six fights and three victories were recorded. Böhme, von Richthofen and Hans Reimann all downed Martinsyde G 100s from No 27 Sqn, but Reimann paid for his fourth victory with his life. It has been widely recorded that 2Lt L F Forbes of No 27 deliberately rammed one of the attacking Albatros fighters which then went down out of control, and this is assumed to have been Reimann. However, historian Alex Imrie provides a different perspective with the following excerpt from *Jasta* 2's war diary;

'Reimann, flying from Velu to Lagnicourt, saw an enemy squadron and attacked a machine that had been separated from the formation, when he was attacked from behind by a Nieuport. Wounded in both thighs, he lost control of his machine and crashed vertically to the ground two kilometres northeast of Noreuil.'

The *Staffel* again decimated a flight of No 27 Sqn Martinsydes four days later. One fell to Boelcke, another was credited to the *Staffel* as a whole and a third made it back with a wounded pilot. The demanding hauptmann was still dissatisfied. 'I have to give my pilots some training', Boelcke wrote.

Günther prepares for take-off in his D I 426/16. His personal initial *G* insignia was painted on the dark-camouflaged fuselage in black, with a white outline. This same aircraft was later flown by Leopold Reimann

'That is not so simple because they are all inspired with such fiery zeal that it is often difficult to put the brake on them. Sometimes I have to turn my heavy batteries on them. I always give them some instructions before we take off, and deal out severe criticism after every flight, and especially after every fight'. His pupils took his critiques happily – von Richthofen would later employ the same methods with the pilots under his own command.

30 September saw von Richthofen's destruction of an FE 2b, but Ltn d R Ernst Diener fell as the third *Staffel* casualty. British ace Capt Albert Ball claimed two 'Rolands' out of control and an Albatros two-seater over Velu, one of which may have been an erroneous description of Diener's D I. *Jasta* 2 had logged 186 combat flights in September, with 21 confirmed victories and four more unconfirmed, at the cost of three pilots.

Boelcke raised his own tally to 30 on 1 October, but again triumph was muted by tragedy. On the 4th Böhme penned another letter;

'Unfortunately our young circle has also been thinned. The *Staffel* has already lost four brave comrades in air fights, among them Hans Reimann, our superb pianist. The last to fall, three days ago, is my friend (Herwarth) Phillips, whose parents in Africa were almost my next-door neighbours – shot down by an idiotic chance hit from a flak gun. We were all in his immediate vicinity.'

New replacements included Ltn Bodo *Freiherr* von Lyncker (a friend of von Richthofen's from their student pilot days) and Ltn d R Erich König from Bavarian Fl Abt 6. Oblt Stefan Kirmaier arrived from *Jasta* 6 on 9 October. Already highly decorated, the 27-year-old Kirmaier had scored three victories in *KEK* Jametz – he would also serve as the unit's technical officer. Also posted in from *Jasta* 6 was Ltn Karl Heinrich Otto

Ltn d R Hans Imelmann achieved his
first victory on 10 October when he
downed a Sopwith 1¹/₂ Strutter.
Imelmann is seen posing at
Lagnicourt with his Albatros D I.
The high pylon or vee-strut centre
section and side-mounted Windhoff
radiator are evident

Büttner, while Ltn Jürgen Sandel arrived from Fl Abt 39. The youngest newcomer was 19-year-old Ltn d R Hans Imelmann (no relation to Max Immelmann – note the different spelling) from Hannover, a veteran of *KEK* Metz.

10 October saw *Jasta* 2 make 31 combat flights, engage in 18 dogfights and score four victories. The young Imelmann made his presence known by downing a Sopwith from the hard-pressed No 70 Sqn. Böhme and Müller both despatched FE 2bs while the *Staffelführer* riddled the DH 2 of 2Lt M J Mare-Montembault of No 32 Sqn. The DH 2 pilot managed to crash-land his fighter near Pozières and escape to the safety of the British trenches.

LUFTSTREITKRÄFTE

At this time *Jasta* 2 and the rest of the German Army Air Service underwent a transformation. A new organisation, the *Luftstreitkräfte,* was born from sweeping changes made on 8 October 1916. The office of *Kommandierenden General der Luftstreitkräfte* (or *Kogenluft*) was created and Generalleutnant Ernst von Hoeppner was appointed to this position.

Ltn Jürgen Sandel arrived at *Jasta* 2 from *Flieger Abteilung* 39 in October 1916. His Albatros D I 431/16 was marked with a black *S* on the fuselage. Note the small holes around the rim of the propeller spinner – possibly a unique feature. Sandel and von Richthofen both shot down BE 12 aircraft on 16 October, but Sandel failed to receive confirmation for his

Besides Boelcke, *Jasta* 2 pilots von Richthofen and Offz Stv Leopold Reimann also achieved victories on 16 October. Here, Leopold Reimann poses with D I 426/16, which was previously flown by Günther. A crude *R* has been painted on to the original print to indicate Reimann's 'ownership' of this aircraft, but it is unknown if such a marking was ever actually applied to the fighter

Fine weather on 16 October brought out aircraft from both sides. At 1405 hrs the *Staffel* swept through the area around Thiépval, and Leopold Reimann sent down a BE 2c for his third confirmed claim. Twenty minutes later Boelcke was credited with another BE east of Hébuterne. At 1700 hrs, von Richthofen, Sandel and two others attacked a flight of seven BE 12s from No 19 Sqn above Bertincourt. Von Richthofen shot down 2Lt J Thompson, while Capt C Tidswell was also killed, being claimed by Sandel – for some reason the latter did not receive confirmation of his victory, however. Forty-five minutes after this, Boelcke attacked the DH 2 of Lt P A Langan-Byrne DSO, commander of No 24 Sqn's 'C' Flight. The German ace later recalled;

'We ran into a squadron of six Vickers single-seaters south of Bapaume at 1745 hrs. We went into some fine turns. The English leader, with

streamers on his machine, came just right for me. I settled him with my first attack – apparently the pilot was killed, for the machine spun down. I watched it down until it crashed about a kilometre east of Beaulencourt. This was a very good day for my *Staffel*. The total since September is 37 victories, although we have had a lot of bad weather lately. They are really splendid, clever gentlemen – my *Staffel*.'

These were indeed heady days for *Jasta* 2. 'I have never found a more beautiful hunting ground than in the skies at the Battle of the Somme', recounted von Richthofen. 'The first Englishmen came very early in the morning, and the last disappeared after the sun had gone down. It was wonderful! Not a mission without a fight.'

One of those fights on 17 October resulted in the destruction of two FE 2bs from No 11 Sqn by Kirmaier and Boelcke. Kirmaier left this account of his fourth victory, translated by Adam Wait;

'We were all ready to take off in the morning at around 1030 hrs when, quite suddenly, a formation of 17 English aircraft appeared over the field. Everybody ran in the direction of the dugout. I thought to myself that it was safer to be in the air and I dashed off. The formation flew further in the direction of Cambrai, bombed a railway station, and then came towards me. I was 2500 metres up. To the left of me and somewhat lower was a lone Englishman who had dropped his bombs in an especially conscientious way.

On 16 October Hptm Boelcke shot down DH 2 A2542, flown by Lt P A Langan-Byrne of No 24 Sqn, for his 34th successful claim. The RFC pilot was killed, but the nacelle of his DH 2 remained relatively intact, as can be seen in this photograph. Noteworthy is the 'sawtooth' pattern of camouflage paint applied to the underside of the nacelle in the characteristic style of No 24 Sqn

As Boelcke returned from scoring his 34th victory, a photographer was on hand to record the event when the Master's eager students gathered around D II 386/16 as he prepared to exit the aircraft. With their backs turned, it is difficult to be certain about the identities of these men, but it is believed that the pilots are, from left to right, von Richthofen, Stefan Kirmaier, Erwin Böhme, Hans Wortmann (with glasses), Günther (in front of Wortmann), Erich König (in long coat), Max Müller and Höhne. Some historians have had the positions of Böhme and von Richthofen reversed

Fresh from his 34th victory, Hptm Boelcke is assisted by Ltn Günther in removing his flying kit as Erich König, with cigarette, observes at right

Whenever Boelcke returned from another patrol, his eager pupils would ask if he had 'gotten another', to which he would respond, 'Is my chin black?' Here, Boelcke wipes the powder stains from his face (a sure sign that his guns had been fired) following his 34th victory on 16 October. Note the swirled stain on the lower wing – an additional attempt at camouflage, which was also densely applied to the rudder of 386/16 (*A Imrie*)

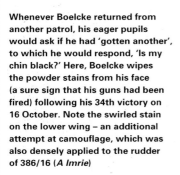

'Above me at about 3000 metres was a tightly knit group of six aircraft. Of course, I had my eye on the lone individual. My faster machine quickly caught up to him. After a perfectly aimed burst from both machine guns, he rolled over on his left wing and rushed downwards. In the dive the observer fell out. The machine itself dashed into a bit of ploughed land near our airfield.'

While some of his pilots were outperforming others, Boelcke showed no favouritism. Von Richthofen noted that everyone who got to know Boelcke felt they were his 'one true friend', and he personally had met about 40 of them! He perceptively realised that Erwin Böhme was really closest to the Master. 'I am proud of the fact that between us a friendship has grown',

Some aircraft aloft has obviously caught the attention of this group of *Jasta* 2 pilots, gathered on the undercarriage of Ltn Sandel's D I 431/16. Seated at left is Sandel, then Manfred von Richthofen with binoculars, Ltn Bodo *Freiherr* von Lyncker with arm raised, and finally Ltn Hans Imelmann

Böhme recorded. 'It is somewhat unique how Boelcke conveys his spirit to each and every one of his students, how he carries all of them away. They follow him wherever he leads. Not one of them would leave him in the lurch. He is a born leader! No wonder his *Staffel* blossoms!'

The *Staffel* blossomed further on the 20th with a bag of four RFC machines. 22 October was another banner day, with Böhme, Imelmann and Reimann each downing one while Boelcke raised his score to 38. However, the *Staffel* lost a valuable asset when Leopold Reimann was wounded after gaining his fifth victory and left for the hospital. He would be killed in a crash as an instructor on 24 January 1917.

On 25 and 26 October the *Staffel* tallied seven victories, with Boelcke and five pilots all contributing. The Master's score now stood at 40 – an astonishing total for the day. Boelcke's *Staffel* had played a large part in the resurgence of German aerial might on the Somme.

BLACK SATURDAY

The immense workload shouldered by Boelcke had taken its toll. 'My hauptmann kept on growing thinner and more serious', recorded his faithful orderly, Fischer. 'The superhuman burden of seven take-offs a day for fights and the worries about the *Staffel* weighed him down. Gen von Below, the commander-in-chief of our army, wanted to send him on leave because he was overworked, but he would not go. When he came home from a flight two days before his death, he said to me, "Fischer, I found an opponent who was a match for me today. There will be hard fighting in the next few days. But no bullet will ever hit me'.

20 October was another successful day as Boelcke, Erwin Böhme and Max Müller all added to their tallies. This *Jasta* 2 foursome includes, from left to right, König, Kirmaier, Böhme and (probably) Günther. On 28 October Böhme suffered his fateful mid-air collision with his friend and commander Boelcke, and Kirmaier would take over the *Staffel*

'The last evening he soon left the mess and came back to his room. "There's too much noise for me", he said. Then Ltn Böhme came in and asked, "Can I keep you company for a bit, hauptmann? There's such a row in the mess". They then sat talking for a long time by the fireside.'

Saturday, 28 October dawned with low clouds, strong winds and occasional showers. Enemy aircraft were reported at 0700 hrs, and Boelcke took off. The *Staffelführer* had reportedly made five flights by early afternoon. Around 1600 hrs Böhme and Boelcke were relaxing with a game of chess, when an urgent call came in for support during an infantry attack. The men tried to hold the exhausted Boelcke back, but he jumped into his D II 386/16 and asked, 'All ready?' The *Jasta* took off and was soon embroiled in a whirling fight with their old foes – two DH 2s of No 24 Sqn, flown by Lt A G Knight and 2Lt A E McKay.

In the midst of the melee, Boelcke and Böhme were both hot on the tail of Knight's fighter. Suddenly, the other DH 2, pursued by von Richthofen, cut in front of them and Böhme and his commander pulled up to evade it. Both had their views blocked by their own wings, and Böhme's undercarriage brushed Boelcke's upper left wing. Böhme wrote, 'It was only a light touch, but at such breakneck speeds that also meant a strong impact. Fate is usually so horribly irrational in its choice'.

Böhme regained control of his Albatros after falling 200 metres, but could only watch helplessly as Boelcke's crippled D II glided down minus a portion of its left wing. Then, according to Böhme, 'He went into an ever steepening glide, and I saw before the landing how he could no longer keep his aircraft facing straightforward, and how he struck the ground near a gun battery'.

Böhme flew back to Lagnicourt, and was so distraught he later did not even remember that he nosed over on landing. The *Staffel* pilots held out some hope, but as they arrived at the crash site, Boelcke's corpse was brought out to them.

The Master's death came as a stunning blow not only to *Jasta* 2, but also to much of the German Army and population. Böhme was at first inconsolable over his part in the fate of his close friend, and commander, but he was a resilient individual and eventually regained his determination

On 24 September 1917, *Jasta* 2 relocated to Lagnicourt, some nine kilometres due north of Bertincourt. Two of the unit's Albatros D I fighters are seen on the flightline at Lagnicourt a month later. The D I at right is probably Ltn Karl Büttner's 391/16 (marked with his *Bü* in white), while Günther's 426/16 is at right. The church steeple of Lagnicourt, which can be seen over the wingtip of the D I at right, made a good landmark for the pilots, and can often be seen in photographs

Erwin Böhme is seen at right, with his visiting brother Gerhard at left, in front of an Albatros D I. Ltn Gerhard Böhme served as a veterinarian in a field artillery regiment

DEBUT OVER THE SOMME

On 31 October 1916, a massive funeral service was held for Oswald Boelcke in Cambrai Cathedral. Here, the funeral procession emerges from the cathedral. Manfred von Richthofen – in fur collar – carries the *Ordenskissen,* the black pillow that displays the dead man's decorations. In the foreground is the gun carriage that would carry Boelcke's coffin

In the wake of Boelcke's death, the mantle of leadership of *Jasta* 2 fell on Oblt Stefan Kirmaier. Here, Kirmaier poses in front of his Albatros D II, which displays leader's streamers wrapped around the interplane struts. Kirmaier's supplemental personal identification was a simple black band painted just ahead of the cross insignia. The fuselage of this machine was either stained or painted a dark colour, but had a light blue underside

to fulfil his duties. Kirmaier took command of the *Staffel*, and his investigation cleared Böhme of any blame.

On 31 October an impressive funeral service was conducted at Cambrai Cathedral. Von Richthofen wrote that the ceremony was 'like that of a reigning prince', and it was his honour to carry Boelcke's medals on his *Ordenskissen* (a black velvet pillow). Amidst the many floral tributes that decorated Boelcke's coffin, two were especially noteworthy. One was inscribed, 'From the British officers who are prisoners of war at Osnabruck, for the opponent we admired and esteemed so highly'. Capt R E Wilson, Boelcke's 20th victim, was one of the airmen responsible. Another wreath had been dropped over the German lines by an RFC pilot who risked his life in doing so – 2Lt T S Green of No 3 Sqn. It read;

'To the memory of Captain Boelcke, our brave and chivalrous opponent. From the English Royal Flying Corps.'

Gen von Below delivered an oration in the name of the Kaiser, and Kirmaier spoke on behalf of *Jasta* 2. Then the coffin was placed on a train and transported to Dessau. There, a massive funeral was conducted on 2 November, attended by high-ranking generals and royalty.

Kirmaier proved a worthy successor to Boelcke. The *Staffel* continued to perform up to the standards set by its founder, with five pilots each tallying a victory on 3 November. On this day, von Richthofen wrote to his mother, 'In six weeks we have six dead and one wounded – two more have lost their nerve. Up to now, my nerves have not yet suffered all the bad luck of the others'. He proved this with the destruction of an FE 2b on the 3rd, while two more fell to Müller for his third and König for his first. Imelmann shot a No 60 Sqn Nieuport down behind the German lines for his fourth *Luftsieg*, and Höhne was also credited with his own number four. Kirmaier brought in a new OzbV at about this time, Oblt Karl Bodenschatz – he was an old comrade of Kirmaier's from their pre-war unit, the 8th Bavarian Infantry Regiment.

Bad weather precluded combat until 9 November, when it resumed in earnest. A force of 16 BE 2c bombers under the protection of 'Fees' from No 11 Sqn, DH 2s from No 29 Sqn and No 60 Sqn Nieuports set out

On 16 November Ltn Karl Büttner of the *Staffel* was brought down behind British lines and captured, along with his intact D I 391/16. His D I, with its prominent *Bü* insignia, became the subject of intense scrutiny by the RFC and the British aeronautical press. Note that the white cross backgrounds on both the fuselage and tail were reduced to produce narrow outlines

on a raid on the ammunition dump at Vraucourt. This aerial armada was intercepted by fighters from *Jagdstaffeln* 1 and 2, resulting in what the official RAF historian called 'the biggest air fight which the war had yet seen'. Kirmaier drove down a bomber, then the ever-aggressive von Richthofen and Imelmann both despatched BEs at around 1030 hrs. Twenty minutes later, No 60 Sqn's pilots were again on the receiving end, as the recently-arrived Ltn d R Hans Wortmann riddled one Nieuport for his first victory and Höhne wounded Lt A D Bell-Irving for his fifth. Later that afternoon Böhme downed his sixth opponent. With his score at eight, von Richthofen received his 'Hohenzollern' on 11 November.

FINAL SOMME PUSH

The Somme offensive was drawing to a close by 13 November, when the final British effort known as the Battle of the Ancre began – the same day Ltn von Lyncker was injured in a crash and left the unit. On 16 November Ltn Karl Büttner's Albatros D I 391/16 was shot down through a single bullet in the radiator during an attack on a BE 2c flown

The first weeks of November continued to bring success for *Jasta* 2, providing good reason for the smiles seen on this group. From left are Stefan Kirmaier, Hans Imelmann, a very casual Manfred von Richthofen (with his famous knobbed walking stick) and Hans Wortmann. Kirmaier brought his score to 11 with four victims in November, von Richthofen also claimed four, Imelmann downed two and Wortmann achieved the first of his two victories. The Albatros D II in the background, with a white band on the nose and light-coloured spinner, seems to have been von Richthofen's

by Capt G A Parker and Lt H E Hervey of No 8 Sqn. Büttner was taken prisoner near Pommies and his D I – the first such aircraft to fall into Allied hands intact – became the subject of considerable study.

17 November was again successful for the *Jasta*, as Höhne destroyed yet another DH 2 from Maj Hawker's No 24 Sqn, killing 2Lt W C Crawford. Three British aircraft were credited on 20 November, two falling to von Richthofen, who had just returned from leave, and another to Kirmaier for his 11th victory. Two days later, Kirmaier's own 'Hohenzollern' was approved, but he would never wear the order.

On the 22nd Kirmaier and four others flew over the lines west of Bapaume. Böhme later recalled the flight (as translated by Peter Kilduff);

'Our British clientele is somewhat intimidated – we must seek them out farther and farther on the other side. Five of us were underway and we were attacked by two big squadrons at the same time over there. Each of us had to handle several opponents. I saw Kirmaier as he hotly pursued a Vickers two-seater, but had several behind him.'

Böhme himself shot down a Morane Parasol from No 3 Sqn, while König accounted for an FE 2b from No 11 Sqn. However, their old DH 2 antagonists of No 24 Sqn were also in the area. 'A' Flight commander Capt J O Andrews slipped within close range of Kirmaier's Albatros and emptied a drum of ammunition into it for his seventh victory. Kirmaier fell with a single bullet in the back of his head, his D II crashing into the British frontlines near Les Boeufs.

Until a new *Staffelführer* could be found, Oblt Bodenschatz would serve as acting commander. In the air, von Richthofen became the *de facto* leader. The very day after Kirmaier's death he would prove his worth in one of the war's most celebrated aerial duels.

Three DH 2s from No 24 Sqn were on a defensive patrol near Bapaume. Kirmaier's victor, Capt Andrews, led the trio, which included Capt R H M S Saundby and – unusually – Maj Lanoe Hawker VC DSO. Hawker was a legend in the RFC, having won the first Victoria Cross given for air combat. He had achieved seven victories in the summer of 1915, but as commander of No 24 Sqn he had not been required to fly. Nonetheless, Hawker flew at every opportunity, and was doing so this day as a last-minute replacement.

Shortly after 1350 hrs Andrews spotted two enemy aircraft and led his flight down, driving the Germans east. He then spotted two patrols of hostile scouts above them and broke off the attack, but then saw that Hawker was still pursuing the first two enemy aeroplanes. Andrews and Saundby followed him eastward and 'were at once attacked by the hostile aircraft, one of which dived onto Maj Hawker's tail'.

Their attackers were von Richthofen and two others from *Jasta* 2. There followed what Andrews' logbook called a 'violent fight', and Richthofen squared off against Hawker as his comrades occupied the other two DH 2 pilots. The two airmen were equally matched. 'I was soon keenly aware that I was not dealing with a beginner', recounted von Richthofen in his autobiography, 'for he did not even dream of breaking off the fight. To be sure, he had a very manoeuvrable crate, but mine climbed better'. The *Kurvenkampf* began as the two circled around after each other, always driven eastward by the wind. Von Richthofen even reported that once Hawker waved at him 'quite cheerfully'.

Jasta 2 lost its second *Staffelführer* in less than a month when Stefan Kirmaier was shot down over Les Boeufs by Capt J O Andrews of No 24 Sqn. The very next day, Manfred von Richthofen avenged Kirmaier's death by bringing down the celebrated commander of No 24 Sqn, Maj Lanoe G Hawker VC DSO

Ltn d R Diether Collin arrived at *Jasta* 2 from *Jasta* 22 in November and would score two of his 13 victories in the *Staffel*. Collin was assigned this Albatros D I, which was painted green on its upper surfaces and marked with his *Co* emblem in white letters with black outlines. This same aircraft was later taken over by the Prussian *Prinz Friedrich Karl*, the acting commander of neighbouring FI Abt (A) 258. The Prince yearned to be a *Jagdflieger*, and sometimes flew with the *Jasta*. Indeed, it is the Prince who is climbing into the cockpit here (*T Phillips*)

The German ace's combat report stated;

'I attacked, together with two other aeroplanes, a Vickers one-seater at 3000 metres altitude. After a long curving fight of three to five minutes, I had forced my adversary down to 500 metres. He now tried to escape, flying to the Front.'

Hawker was forced to make a break for it, and zigzagged westward. Von Richthofen closed in, firing away, then both his guns jammed. He managed to clear the stoppage and 'brought him down after 900 shots'. Hawker was hit in the back of the head and his DH 2 5964 crashed to earth south of Bapaume. Von Richthofen was happy to learn from the statements of RFC prisoners that Hawker was regarded as the 'English Boelcke', for he regarded this fight as the most difficult he had yet experienced.

Hawker was actually the second No 24 Sqn pilot to fall to *Jasta* 2 on 23 November. A few hours earlier, 2Lt H B Begg had been killed by the new *Staffel* pilot Ltn d R Collin. The 23-year-old Diether Collin had only recently transferred in from *Jasta* 22, but he wasted little time. He shot down Begg's DH 2 at 1100 hrs east of Morval for his first accredited success. His second of 13 eventual victories would be yet another No 24 Sqn DH 2 downed little more than a month later, on 26 December. Collin initially flew an Albatros D I painted green, marked with his *Co* legend on the fuselage.

It was also during this period that a 19-year-old pilot destined to make a huge mark in the *Staffel* record was posted to *Jasta* 2. Ltn d R Werner Voss was born on 13 July 1897 in Krefeld, and went to war as a 17-year-old in the 2. *Westfälische Husaren-Regiment* Nr 11. After transferring to aviation and being trained as a pilot, he was posted to *Kasta* 20 of *Kagohl* IV on 10 March 1916. In May he earned his pilot's badge, and was promoted to Ltn d R on 9 September 1917. Voss made an impressive debut just a few days after arriving at *Jasta* 2 when he scored a 'double' on 27 November for his first victories – the same day that Max Müller achieved his fifth.

29 November ushered in the command era of new *Staffelführer* Bavarian Oblt Franz Josef Walz. A regular army officer and prewar

military pilot, 31-year-old Walz had led *Kasta* 2 of *Kagohl* I and had achieved six victories as a two-seater pilot between April and July of 1916. He was wounded on 30 July, and after recovery had trained new pilots at Bavarian FEA 1 in Schleissheim, then returned to *Kagohl* I. By November Walz was placed in charge of forming the new *Jasta* 19, but just three weeks later he got the call to take over *Jasta* 2.

On 5 December the *Jasta* relocated to Pronville aerodrome, southeast of Quéant, and still in the 1. *Armee*. Six days later the *Staffel* received a visit from *Kogenluft* von Hoeppner himself, who promised them better equipment, and took enjoyment in the décor of their officers' mess – two chandeliers made from captured British propellers. Soon after an Imperial decree renamed the unit *Jagdstaffel* 'Boelcke' in honour of its revered founder. From then on this was its preferred title, sometimes shortened to *Jasta* B.

It might be said that von Richthofen brought further closure to the Boelcke story on 20 December when he despatched yet another successful DH 2 pilot. At 1130 hrs von Richthofen led four other pilots down onto a formation of No 29 Sqn pushers above Monchy-au-Bois. All the RFC machines were badly shot up, and von Richthofen killed Capt A G Knight, an eight-victory ace. Knight had previously flown with No 24 Sqn, and he was the pilot that Boelcke and Böhme had been pursuing at the time of their deadly collision. Later that day von Richthofen brought his score to 14 with an FE 2b, with two more claimed by Imelmann and Wortmann.

As 1916 ended, the *Staffel* tally stood at 86 enemy aeroplanes destroyed – far more than any other *Jasta*. Von Richthofen had emerged as its premier living ace with 15 victories. The first weeks of 1917 quickly brought about some changes for *Jasta* 2, however. One of these was the gradual arrival of sesquiplane Albatros D IIIs. On 4 January von Richthofen met the heightened benchmark for the *Pour le Mérite* by downing his 16th opponent. Only two days later he was informed that he had been named commander of his own unit, *Jasta* 11. Von Richthofen left his cherished *Staffel* with mixed feelings, but he was determined to pass on Boelcke's teachings to a new group of unblooded pilots. Thus *Jasta* B continued on into 1917 with new aircraft, but without its top-scoring pilot, under a commander who had not achieved a victory in nearly six months.

Four Albatros machines of *Jasta* 2 are lined up on Lagnicourt airfield. Von Richthofen appears at left in the light-coloured pullover sweater, just in front of his Albatros D II. The other three machines are D I fighters

'BLOODY APRIL'

The Winter of 1916-17 was one of the coldest on record, and aerial operations were subsequently limited. The water-cooled in-line engines of Albatros fighters froze up with discouraging regularity, and if the aircraft did get aloft, their bone-chilled pilots often found their guns frozen as well. *Jasta* B recorded only three victories in January and suffered several misfortunes.

Von Richthofen was not the only member of the 'old guard' to depart from the unit in January. The exhausted Erwin Böhme was ordered to go on leave on the 9th as he was 'in need of rest'. He did not protest, and was soon indulging in his favourite pastime of hiking in the Bavarian Alps. After failing to score any victories in three months, Ltn Sandel was posted out to a two-seater unit on the 9th. The next day Otto Höhne was badly wounded in the upper arm and chest during a fight with Sopwiths and left for a lengthy convalescence. Max Müller was posted to the Württemberg *Jasta* 28 on 19 or 20 January and Collin left for *Jasta* 22 at the same time.

The *Jasta* suffered a staggering blow on 23 January when two pilots were killed within 35 minutes. Hans Imelmann probably felt his seventh victory was close at hand when he pounced on a BE 2 over Miraumont at 1405 hrs. The crew of Capt J C McMillan and 2Lt Hopkins of No 4 Sqn turned the tables on their attacker, however, Hopkins' fire setting Imelmann's Albatros aflame. Some 30 minutes later McMillan and Hopkins' BE was attacked *again*, this time by *Jasta* B newcomer Vzfw Paul Ostrop. He had been with the *Staffel* for little more than two weeks. As he concentrated on stalking the two-seater, a DH 2 came to the rescue and downed Ostrop. The DH 2 pilot was Lt E C Pashley from the *Jasta* nemesis, No 24 Sqn.

When he heard of this day's losses, Böhme wrote, 'I received the very sorrowful message that our Imelmann, the youngest in the *Staffel*, fell on 23 January. He was a combat comrade without fear or blame'.

Jasta 2 reportedly received its first Albatros D IIIs on 7 January, but D IIs and D Is remained in use for some time to come. It was one of the new D IIIs that was lost next, along with a new pilot. Flugmt Gustav Kinkel had been posted to *Jasta* 'Boelcke' on 13 January – as his rank indicates, he was a naval pilot gaining experience with an Army unit.

On 25 January Kinkel was flying his D III south of Bapaume when he also had the ill fortune to encounter a flight of No 24 Sqn's DH 2s. Lt A E McKay shot down the Albatros west of Combles for his fourth victory, describing it in his report as a 'single-seat Albatros with Nieuport struts and planes. Large K on side of fuselage'. Kinkel was lucky to survive as a PoW. His aircraft was the first D III to fall into Allied hands, and its serial number was recorded by the British as 1982/16. However, Alex Imrie has noted that the *Jasta* 'Boelcke' war diary records the same number for Imelmann's machine destroyed two days before! Obviously someone transcribed a number incorrectly.

In the wake of these serious losses, *Jasta* 'Boelcke' was fortunate to have at least one extremely capable replacement. At the end of January Oblt Adolf *Ritter* von Tutschek arrived at the *Staffel*.

The highly decorated Bavarian Oblt Adolf *Ritter* von Tutschek arrived at *Jasta* 2 – now known as *Jasta* 'Boelcke' – in late January 1917. On 6 March he added his name to the *Staffel* logbook with his first confirmed claim, and would score two more with the unit before being posted to *Jasta* 12. This photograph shows him after he had won the *Pour le Mérite* in August 1917

Born into a military family on 16 May 1891 in Ingolstadt, he joined the 3. *Bayerischen Infanterie-Regiment* in 1910 and was commissioned shortly before the war. After considerable action on the Western Front, von Tutschek was transferred to Russia as a company commander. For his valiant actions on the Eastern Front he was awarded the Bavarian Knight's Cross of the Military Max-Joseph Order, earning the title of *Ritter* von Tutschek. By March 1916 he had been promoted to oberleutnant, and he was then gassed while serving at Verdun.

Following recovery, von Tutschek was accepted for pilot training, and in late October 1916 he was posted to Fl Abt 6b, where he served with distinction. Von Tutschek and his observer claimed to have downed two aircraft on 26 December 1916, and he was particularly angered when these victories were disallowed in spite of all the eyewitness reports he had submitted – they went instead to two fighter pilots. Thus, the Bavarian was eager to make his mark as a *Jagdflieger* when he arrived at Pronville.

Von Tutschek's diary records four test flights in D I 1708/16 on 26 January 1917. He made his first frontline patrol the next day, followed by a test hop in D I 438/16 on the 28th and two patrols on the 29th.

The unit's fortunes began to turn around on 1 February when Albatros pilots tangled with four DH 2s of No 29 Sqn in the afternoon. Werner Voss locked onto the pusher flown by Capt A P V Daly and shot up its engine and wounded the pilot in the shoulder. Daly managed to glide down to a landing near Essarts, where he was captured. Voss later visited the pilot in the hospital, presenting him with cigars and his visiting card.

Upon hearing of the casualties his unit had suffered, Erwin Böhme cut short his leave. Well-rested and back to his old form, Böhme shot down two aeroplanes on his first patrol on 4 February. At 1505 hrs he wounded the pilot of a No 32 Sqn DH 2 for his tenth victory, and followed this up with a BE from No 15 Sqn only 25 minutes later. At 1540 hrs Voss sent an artillery-spotting BE from No 16 Sqn down in flames, its pilot, 2Lt H Martin-Massey, surviving despite severe burns – its observer, 2L N Vernham, was killed, however. Ten minutes earlier Erich König had claimed a BE from the same squadron for his fourth 'kill'. König's victory was not achieved single-handedly, however. Von Tutschek was probably referring to this action when he wrote;

'I was terribly angered. I sat on the tail of a BE from 3000 metres down to 1800 and powdered him from close range. Just when he began to trundle downward, Ltn König came and gave him the final dosage.'

In the competitive world of the *Jagdstaffeln* there were no shared victories, and this one went to König.

However, there were worse developments than a simple victory dispute. Ltn Christian von Scheele (who had arrived at *Jasta* 2 only days before) failed to return from this day's combat. An experienced pilot, he had flown in *Kagohl* II along with Böhme and von Richthofen. Once again, DH 2 pilot Lt Pashley of No 24 Sqn accounted for one of the Boelcke *Staffel*. Von Scheele apparently dived on five FE 2bs from No 22 Sqn but was attacked by Pashley, who riddled the Albatros from just 20 metres.

VOSS IN THE ASCENDANCY

Werner Voss was clearly emerging as the new star of the *Staffel*. On 10 February he brought his total to six during a *Jasta* attack on a patrol

Another pilot rapidly building up his score in *Jasta* 'Boelcke' in early 1917 was 19-year-old Werner Voss. He is seen here with a 'Wanderer' motorcycle. Voss won his own 'Blue Max' on 8 April 1917 after piling up 24 victories in quick succession

When Ltn Fritz Otto Bernert arrived at *Jasta* 'Boelcke' in late February, he already had a formidable reputation with at least seven victories and the ribbon of the 'Hohenzollern' on his tunic. He scored his first victory with his new unit on 24 March, and would start off 'Bloody April' by torching a balloon on the 1st, followed by a Nieuport the next day and two more gasbags on the 3rd. This Sanke Card portrait shows him after his 'Blue Max' was awarded on 23 April

of No 32 Sqn DH 2s. In this fight Böhme was credited with a 'Vickers two-seater' for his 12th score. However, as he tried for his ominous number 13 the next day, ill fortune caught up with him. Two days later Böhme explained to his girlfriend Annamarie;

'I find myself in a field hospital, because the day before yesterday a malevolent Englishman, who was defeated theoretically, shot me maliciously in the left arm. It was a Sopwith two-seater, which I had already fought down so far that he intended to land. For that reason, I spared him in a burst of sportsman-like grace – that's what I get for my courtesy! I am only angry about having to leave my *Staffel* in the lurch just as the Spring hunt has begun.'

Böhme received his 'Hohenzollern' during his recovery.

Now König and Wortmann were the only pilots left in the unit who had once flown under Boelcke. Some replacements did arrive during February though, among them Ltn d R Johannes Wintrath on the 20th. The veteran König contributed three victories in February, but no less than eight more were the handiwork of Werner Voss. He frequently scored in 'doubles', and on the 25th he downed two DH 2s while König vanquished another. These victories brought the *Staffel* total to a momentous 100, but Voss was just getting started. 27 February saw him destroy two of the hapless BEs, bringing his tally to eleven.

Fortunately, more Albatros D IIIs were becoming available, as von Tutschek recorded;

'After a month as an air fighter I've made 42 flights, among which 35 were offensive patrols. And all without a personal victory, although *Jasta* "Boelcke" registered 14 air victories, despite the fact that the enemy has been hanging back. Up until 16 February 1917, I flew an Albatros D I and then D III 1925/16.'

On 23 February Ltn Fritz Otto Bernert arrived at Pronville. Less than two weeks short of his 24th birthday, he was a native of Ratibor, Upper Silesia. Fighting in the infantry on the Western Front, he had suffered a bayonet thrust in December 1914 that left him with limited use of his left arm. However, he was considered fit enough for the air service! After serving as an observer, Bernert received his pilot's training at the Halberstadt and Hannover schools. In *KEK* Vaux he destroyed a Nieuport in April 1916, and remained with the unit as it was transformed into *Jasta* 4, chalking up its first victory on 6 September. On 9 November Bernert downed three aircraft in one flight, taking his tally to seven.

MARCH 1917

March would be Werner Voss' breakout month – out of 15 opponents vanquished by *Jasta* 'Boelcke', 11 fell to the hussar from Krefeld. Still noticeably absent from the log was the name of *Staffelführer* Walz, who had not tallied a single victory in four months as a *Jagdflieger*.

On 4 March Voss subtracted a BE 2d from the strength of No 8 Sqn, the crew perishing in their flaming aircraft. Two days later the *Jasta* war diary entry reported that 11 machines were airworthy, and that 15 combat flights were made – five aerial battles occurred, with two successful. Voss downed DH 2 7941 from No 32 Sqn, Capt H G Southon being lucky to survive as a wounded PoW. Von Tutschek finally achieved his first *confirmed* success on this day in Albatros D II 1994/16. He penned the following report;

'At 1630 hrs the "Boelcke" *Staffel* attacked a Vickers squadron which was flying eastward over the front at 2800 metres altitude. I took on an English one-seater over Beugnatre and forced him away from his squadron in a northerly direction. After about 100 rounds the enemy craft went down in a dive, but caught himself when 600 metres from the ground, whereupon I immediately attacked him again and forced him down in a dogfight north of Beugnatre. The occupant was captured by *Fusilier-Regiment* Nr 90. No other German machine entered the combat.

'The Vickers one-seater had a rotary engine and a built-in machine gun. The pilot was Lt M J Mare-Montembault, who was taken prisoner unwounded.'

Werner Voss collected eight victories in February, followed by eleven more in March. At some point he was assigned the Albatros D III seen here, which he soon decorated with the help of his mechanics Karl Timm and Christian Rüser. Here, Voss puts the finishing touches on his white-outlined red heart emblem. Just aft of the heart was a white swastika. Timm suggested the swastika looked rather bare, so he added a laurel wreath around it, with a blue bow at the bottom

Mare-Montembault of No 32 Sqn had survived being shot down by Boelcke back on 10 October.

The *Staffel* war diary noted that a new airfield was being prepared at Eswars, just north of Cambrai – the *Jasta* would settle in there on 14 March. Von Tutschek recorded that his quarters in Eswars were 'quite charming', and as room décor he had the four-bladed propeller from his first victory, as well as its rotary engine, which was being converted into a 'nine cylinder chandelier'.

Voss continued his March rampage with more doubles – two downed on the 11th and another pair on 17 March. On the latter date he received his 'Hohenzollern'. Not one to rest on his laurels, Voss destroyed two BEs on the 18th to bring his total to 19. The downing of the second of these two aircraft became something of a legend in *Jagdflieger* lore. A first-hand account by Voss has survived;

'While I was continuously spiralling upwards over Neuville together with Ltn Wortmann, who was always behind me, a BE two-seater came towards us somewhat to the north and much higher, and then continued in a southerly direction. As I later determined, he was engaged in artillery spotting. I had soon reached the height of the BE and approached closer to him from behind.

'The opponent shot at me from about 200 metres distance and dived steeply back to his front. Because of my continual fire, which I began at a distance of about 100 metres, and which I held until I was right behind him, the BE went into banks and spirals. I stayed behind him almost continuously, and could get off good bursts at the closest distance.

'After I had followed him down with many banks, suddenly a second Albatros from my *Staffel* dived in between us from the left, and a collision almost happened. This Albatros turned upwards once more, while I followed the opponent all the way down till right over the ground and shot at him. During a forced landing, the BE (No 5770) got quite smashed up.

Voss' D III is seen here freshly decorated, engine mechanic Timm standing in front with the paint pot, while Christian Rüser sits in the cockpit. Note the delicate white-outlined blue ribbon beneath the laurel wreath. Later on, the heart insignia would be repeated on top of the fuselage. By this time the white tail with a black border at the leading edge had been adopted as the *Staffel* marking of *Jasta* 'Boelcke'

'I recognised the cavalrymen running about by their steel helmets and field caps to be Germans, and so I decided to land on a grassy area nearby. Here, I discovered that these cavalrymen were the last Germans before the advancing enemy, whose patrol was close by. I took out the two Lewis machine guns from the aircraft and had them brought back to the First Company of I R 107, to be stored there. Then I shot the fuel tanks of the BE, set it on fire and took off again.'

Voss' narrow escape from approaching British troops became an oft-repeated story. What he failed to mention was the fate of the BE crew. Capt G Thorne was mortally wounded, but still managed to land the crippled BE. The observer, Lt F Van Baerle, later only recalled that as the crew sat on the ground, an Albatros – presumably Voss – strafed them. They were shortly taken into captivity, but Thorne died that night.

That same 18 March, *Jasta* B received a congratulatory letter from *Kogenluft* von Hoeppner. 'It has been reported to me that *Jagdstaffel* "Boelcke" has shot down the 100th aeroplane in air combat since its

As noted, *Prinz* Friedrich Karl of Prussia was flying with Fl Abt (A) 258, but often flew an Albatros with *Jasta* 'Boelcke'. The Prince is seen here at left, fastening his flying helmet, as he prepares for flight in his D I, which still displays Collin's *Co* insignia. He would fly for the last time with the *Staffel* on 21 March

Photographs of the Albatros D I in flight are rare. Here is *Prinz* Friedrich Karl taking off in his D I, formerly flown by Collin of *Jasta* 'Boelcke'. Soon after this shot was taken, the Prince had Collin's insignia overpainted with the Death's Head emblem of his old *Leib-Husaren-Regiment* Nr 1 on the fuselage and spinner

founding. A success that stands as yet unequalled!' Von Hoeppner noted that Boelcke had fallen, but 'his spirit lives on in the whole *Fliegertruppe,* just as it lives on in the *Jagdstaffel* which bears his proud name'. Living up to that heritage, Voss and Bernert destroyed two RE 8s from No 59 Sqn the next day.

Jasta B attracted its share of celebrity guests, including *Prinz* Friedrich Karl of Prussia, a second cousin to Kaiser Wilhelm. He had served in the *Leib-Husaren-Regiment* Nr 1, a famous 'Death's Head Hussar' regiment, and was renowned as a dashing sportsman. In October 1916 he transferred to aviation, and by March 1917 was acting commander of Fl Abt (A) 258. Like many two-seater pilots, the Prince yearned for the glory of a *Jagdflieger.* He often visited the nearby field of *Jasta* 'Boelcke', and plans were made for him to transfer to the *Staffel* – he had been given the Albatros D I formerly flown by Collin, and sometimes flew with the *Jasta.*

On 21 March 1917, the Prince joined a *Kette* (flight) from the *Staffel* on a patrol that took off at 1630 hrs. Von Tutschek takes up the story;

'The clouds were hanging at 500 to 600 metres when Voss, Wortmann and I, in succession, found a hole in the clouds over Cambrai and climbed through the mountainous mists. We found beneath us a sea of clouds once we were through, while above us was the most beautiful of blue skies. Ltn Voss was up ahead with the leader, and we followed closely behind.

'As I glanced backward I suddenly spied a strange Albatros to the left, coming toward us. I quickly recognised it as the green Albatros D I of Prince Friedrich Karl of Prussia as he joined us, happily waving his hand. The Prince commanded a Fl Abt, but was to join our *Staffel* in the near future. In the meantime, he was practising on an Albatros from our *Staffel.* He had painted a large skull on both sides of the fuselage and the same on propeller boss. The prince was a frequent visitor, and we liked him a lot.

'Over Arras, we went down in steep spirals hoping to head off an artillery spotter, but there were none. So back we flew just under the clouds over the newly constructed Siegfried Line positions toward the south. Five of us were now in the flight. Voss, Prince Karl, Walz, Wintrath and I. It was clear that we shouldn't become involved in a dogfight as the prevailing strong east wind would surely push us westward. Despite that, our leader (Walz) and Voss turned toward four Vickers *Gitterrumpf* (lattice-fuselage) single-seaters that were also flying just under the clouds at our altitude over Lagnicourt. Ltn Wintrath and I followed and the dance began.

'I went after an Englishman who instantly headed for the clouds just as additional aircraft were coming out of them. The same thing happened to Voss. When I looked back, I noticed the green Albatros of the Prince nearing the ground and spiralling, closely followed by two other enemy aircraft. While Prince Friedrich Karl was in the process of finishing off an Englishman, he was attacked by a second one who shot up his motor so that his only recourse was an immediate landing.

'He climbed out, and while running toward our lines, collapsed. The shots from an Englishman, as we found out later, had ended his life-or-death run as he was struck on the lower torso.'

The Prince had been shot down by DH 2 pilot Lt C Pickthorne of No 32 Sqn. Wounded in the right foot, Friedrich Karl landed between the lines and tried to run for the German trenches, but was shot in the spine

A prized trophy, the fuselage of *Prinz Friedrich Karl's* D I with his Death's Head marking, is surrounded by Australian and French troops after he was shot down on 21 March 1917 – the Prince succumbed to his wounds on 6 April. This was an early D I from the initial prototype series (possibly 384/16), and was fitted with the nose expansion tank instead of the usual triangular tank (*P M Grosz*)

by Australian troops. The Australians brought him to their lines and towed the Albatros fuselage back as well. The Prince was well cared for in captivity but died from his wounds on 6 April.

The *Jasta* transferred to a new airfield at Proville, by Cambrai (not to be confused with Pronville, by Quéant), on the 23rd, and Voss continued to add to his tally whilst flying from the new base. During a late afternoon flight on 24 March, he found an FE 2b from No 23 Sqn on a photographic reconnaissance mission. Voss quickly killed the observer and wounded the pilot, Sgt E P Critchley, who still managed to force land the 'Fee' behind British lines near Achiet-le-Grand. With plenty of fuel and ammunition left, Voss kept hunting, and 20 minutes later latched onto a BE 2, probably from No 8 Sqn, and was again successful in destroying it. Bernert received credit for another victory at about the same time.

On 31 March von Tutschek gained his second official victory;

'Today, at 0900 hrs in Albatros D III 2004/16, a successful air combat was fought in the vicinity of Loos, northwest of Lens, against a Nieuport single-seater. West of Lens at 3500 metres altitude, I attacked a Nieuport which was close behind an Albatros two-seater. Immediately, the Nieuport let up his pursuit of the Albatros two-seater, which was going down in a steep glide, and attempted to outclimb Ltn König and I, but I managed to get behind him. After 150 shots, the machine suddenly stood on its nose, tumbled over and went into the ground almost vertically.'

'BLOODY APRIL' BEGINS

April 1917 would be remembered grimly as 'Bloody April' in the annals of the RFC due to the heavy losses suffered during the Arras Offensive that would commence on the 9th. The first day of April began auspiciously for *Jasta* B. At 1045 hrs Bernert used the cloud cover to slip across the lines and

Adolf von Tutschek was credited with his second victory on the last day of March 1917, and contributed to *Jasta* 'Boelcke's' tally in 'Bloody April' with an FE 2b captured on the 6th. Von Tutschek's lighter side is evident in this view, in which he cheerfully poses with a *Staffel* mascot (complete with cigarette!) carefully placed on the fuselage of an Albatros D III. Von Tutschek had a penchant for wearing captured British flying gear, and here he sports RFC 'fug boots'. The D III displays the *Jasta* 'Boelcke' unit emblem of a white tail, with a black-bordered white band serving as the pilot's personal marking (*A Imrie*)

burn the balloon of the 4th KB Section. About an hour later Voss struck yet again, surprising an artillery-spotting BE 2e from No 15 Sqn. His first bullets struck the pilot, Australian Capt A Wynne, in the leg, and on his second pass he killed the observer, Lt A Mackenzie. Wynne managed to crash the BE just inside the British lines, and survived a strafing run by the exuberant Voss.

April was costly for the *Jagdflieger* as well, however. The second day of the month was Erich König's 27th birthday, but he would not see 28. On a mid-morning patrol *Jasta* B tangled with a group of No 57 Sqn FE 2bs. The courageous RFC gunners' fire sent König's Albatros down in flames. At almost the same time Ltn d R Hans Wortmann was also killed, falling near Vitry-Cambrai. When Erwin Böhme heard the news, he mournfully noted that he and von Richthofen were now the only members of Boelcke's original group left alive.

Nonetheless, Voss and Bernert were doing their best to keep *Jasta* B in the news. Bernert recorded one of his feats;

'On 3 April I was returning from a combat patrol when I spotted two enemy balloons and immediately flew to my airfield, intending to get everything ready for a systematic attack. I had my machine filled with the necessary fuel, got my machine guns in working order and immediately ascended once more. I found the balloon at 800 metres. I was met with heavy cannon, machine gun and artillery fire. In spite of that, my attack was successful. In the next instant, the balloon was ablaze. The enemy shells were now exploding behind, below, beside and close above me.

'I allowed myself to sideslip over on one wing and feigned being shot down. I levelled my machine again, and at the right moment flew toward the second balloon some eight kilometres southwest of Bapaume, and about 14 kilometres beyond the Siegfried Line. The second balloon crew had observed the attack and downing of the first balloon. The enemy recognised my intentions, pulled the balloon down to a low height and began to haul it in. Despite this fact, I proceeded to the attack at the height of only 200 metres. I was heavily fired upon from all sides.

'When I was unable to perceive any immediate effect after my first attack, I went down another 50 metres. My situation was extremely critical, as my guns had jammed right at the crucial moment. However, I was fortunate enough to quickly clear the stoppage and I fired on the balloon with both machine guns, and the result was that this one too now went up in flames. I put my machine into a steep climb because of the shells that were bursting all around me.

'On my flight back, five enemy aircraft that had appeared in the meantime blocked my way. I peeled off in a southerly direction, and at a height of 100 metres found myself over the English trenches, from which I was heavily fired upon as well. I myself remained uninjured, returned to the airfield and reported my success with satisfaction.'

On 6 April – Good Friday – von Tutschek and Voss were relaxing at Proville when suddenly an FE 2b was sighted at 1600 metres. Both quickly took off and raced after the two-seater, catching up with it over Bourlon Wood. Von Tutschek in his black Albatros D III opened fire simultaneously with Voss, putting the engine out of commission with about 60 hits. The FE landed near Anneux, and Voss and von Tutschek tossed a coin to see who would get the victory – von Tutschek wrote that, 'Since I am unlucky in love, the *Gitterschwanz* (lattice-tail) was mine'.

Still a week short of his 20th birthday, Voss was not done for the day. A little over an hour later he notched up his 24th claim, and Bernert destroyed an RE 8 from No 59 Sqn near Roeux as his 14th victory. On Easter Sunday (8 April) the award of Voss' *Pour le Mérite* was announced. He soon left on the customary leave, and therefore was home for his 20th birthday on the 13th. Voss would miss out on the feeding frenzy that took place during the rest of April, but this left the field open for Bernert. On the 7th he had despatched a Nieuport 23 from No 29 Sqn. He quickly followed this up with a double achieved on the 8th, one of them a new Bristol F 2A Fighter from No 48 Sqn.

BATTLE OF ARRAS

After three weeks of preparatory bombardment, the Battle of Arras began on 9 April 1917. At 0530 hrs the greatest concentration of artillery yet assembled opened up, and the British attack against the German 6. and 27. *Armee* Fronts was launched in snow and low drizzle. *Jasta* 'Boelcke' was located to the south of the battlefront, and did not score on this day or the next.

More new faces were showing up at the *Staffel,* and some would play a role in April. Back in March, Ltn d R Hermann Frommherz had arrived.

Ltn d R Hermann Frommherz was posted to *Jasta* 'Boelcke' in March 1917, and would score his first confirmed victory on 11 April with a SPAD, followed by a BE 2c only three days later. Here, Frommherz poses with his mechanics and his *'Blaue Maus'* Albatros. The D III was painted pale blue and had the *Staffel* marking of a white tail and the pilot's personal emblem of diagonal black/white bands

The 25-year-old hailed from Waldshut, in Baden, and had flown in *Kasta* 20 of *Kagohl* IV at Verdun and the Somme. He then went to Romania with *Kasta* 20 and then to Macedonia in December 1916, before his assignment to *Jasta* B. A friend and flying mate of Frommherz in *Kasta* 20 was Ltn d R Friedrich 'Fritz' Kempf, who showed up at the *Jasta* in early April. Kempf was born in Freiburg im Breisgau on 9 May 1894, and had flown in Macedonia and Rumania along with Frommherz – he had just received his Iron Cross 1st Class on 20 March. Posted to *Jasta* B about this same time were Ltns Hans Eggers and Rolf *Freiherr* von Lersner.

Jasta B re-entered the scoring column on 11 April. At 0900 hrs Frommherz forced down SPAD VII A6690 of No 23 Sqn near Cuvillers for his all-important first victory – pilot 2Lt Roche was made a PoW. Some three hours later Bernert was back in action, contributing a 'Vickers' and a Morane to the day's bag. The No 3 Sqn Morane P came down near Lagnicourt, and both crewmen died. Only three days later Frommherz again succeeded in bringing a British aircraft down in German lines, this time a BE 2 from No 10 Sqn. The two-seater was being flown without an observer, and its pilot, 2Lt Holmes, was taken prisoner.

April was clearly Bernert's best month. With 19 victories, he received his 'Blue Max' on 23 April, and on the 24th he accomplished a singular coup. At 0730 hrs Bernert led the *Staffel* down out of the sun onto a formation of Sopwith two-seaters from No 70 Sqn that were conducting a dawn reconnaissance patrol – his accurate fire set one of them afire.

Within minutes Bernert spotted five BE 2e bombers from No 9 Sqn above Bohain, all flying without observers in order to carry extra bombs. In five lethal minutes Bernert shot down three of them (only one pilot survived as a PoW). Still not satisfied, he sighted one of the new DH 4s

The highly capable OzbV (adjutant or special duties officer) of *Jasta* 'Boelcke', Oblt Karl Bodenschatz, is seen kneeling at centre with a *Staffel* mascot named 'Joffre'. He is flanked by Ltn Bernert (right) and Ltn Hans Eggers, who arrived in April. Behind Bodenschatz can be seen Frommherz' pale blue D III, and the nose of Kempf's Albatros is just visible at extreme right (*Prien Album*)

Otto Bernert capped off his string of successes in April in a spectacular manner. According to most sources, Bernert received his *Pour le Mérite* on the 23rd, with his score standing at 19. As if to prove he had earned it, Bernert went on a rampage on the 24th, becoming the first German airman to score five victories in a single day. Here, he poses with a *Jasta* 'Boelcke' Albatros D III. He reportedly had somewhat limited use of his left arm due to an old bayonet wound, and here that limb is tucked into his trouser pocket (*Prien Album*)

from No 55 Sqn at 0850 hrs, and forced the bomber down near Doullens with a wounded pilot and dead observer. His shooting spree took only 20 minutes, and he had done what no other pilot on either side had yet accomplished. There were disputes with flak crews and a *Jasta* 12 pilot to be settled, but Bernert would eventually be credited with five victories.

Before the month was out one more *Jasta* B pilot would leave his first mark on the enemy. The *Nachrichtenblatt* (an official weekly summary of Army aviation activity) records Fritz Kempf as having achieved his first victory on 29 April by despatching a BE at Le Pavé, but other sources cite 30 April as the date. Kempf would serve long and dutifully with the *Jasta* and down three more opponents. *Jasta* B had officially accounted for 21 enemy aeroplanes in April – the only units to inflict more damage were *Jasta* 5 with 32 victories and *Jasta* 11 with an astonishing 89.

It seemed the recurring destiny of *Jasta* B to lose its best pilots to the command of other *Staffeln*. On 28 April Adolf von Tutschek was notified he had been named leader of *Jasta* 12. He wrote, 'I was with *Jagdstaffel* "Boelcke" for a little over three months. In that time I flew 140 missions, of which 120 were offensive patrols. Of these, five combats met with

April also saw the arrival of Ltn d R Friedrich 'Fritz' Kempf at *Jasta* 'Boelcke', and he would score his initial victory on the 29th of that same month. Here, Kempf smiles from the cockpit of the Albatros D III he eventually flew at the *Staffel*. It displayed the unit's white tail and a dark fuselage, marked with a lengthwise white arrow emblem (*P M Grosz*)

Having missed the killing time of 'Bloody April' due to his leave, Werner Voss returned to *Jasta* 'Boelcke' on 5 May and picked up where he left off. On the 7th he downed one of No 56 Sqn's new SE 5 fighters. Here, Voss poses in the shade of his Albatros D III, now displaying the heart emblem on top of the fuselage

success, but only three of them were confirmed'. Only two days later Bernert, too, was transferred out to take over *Jasta* 6. Fortunately Voss soon returned and quickly picked up where he had left off, reaching the quarter century mark on 7 May.

No 56 Sqn had arrived at the Front in April with the new SE 5 fighter (see *Osprey Aircraft of the Aces 78 SE 5/5a Aces of World War 1* for further details), and counted among its pilots the celebrated Capt Albert Ball. On the fateful afternoon of the 7th, 11 SE 5s took off into thick banks of low clouds, and a confused series of fights followed. 2Lt R M Chaworth-Musters of 'B' Flight was seen to leave his formation and enter a cloud

bank in pursuit of an aeroplane. The 19-year-old RFC pilot was shot down by Voss at 1915 hrs at Etaing for his 25th tally. Other No 56 Sqn airmen ran into *Jasta* 11, and two more pilots were wounded and Albert Ball was killed when he became disoriented and crashed – a terrible blow to the RFC.

Voss was clearly at the top of his game, but with Bernert and von Tutschek gone, he may have felt as if he was carrying *Jasta* B's burden all by himself. Hptm Walz was no doubt a capable officer, but he was not an inspiring *Staffelführer* who led his unit in victories like Boelcke or von Richthofen.

On 9 May Voss clearly demonstrated his own deadly proficiency with a 'hat trick'. At 1400 hrs he located a No 52 Sqn BE 2e on an artillery-spotting mission over Havrincourt and shot it to pieces, scattering the wreckage over a large area. Three hours later, Voss was again airborne and led *Jasta* B against a patrol of FEs of No 22 Sqn, escorted by Sopwith Pups from No 54 Sqn. He singled out Pup A6174, flown by Lt Hadrill, and tenaciously hounded it down to the ground, shooting up the fuel tank and engine. Voss then led six others against the FE formation. The two-seaters were forced down to 2000 ft, and Voss and two others attacked the trailing machine – they compelled the pusher to land behind German lines southwest of Hesdin, and 2Lts C Furlonger and C Lane were quickly captured.

Werner Voss was obviously riding high. With his score standing at 28, he was von Richthofen's closest competitor for the title of top-scoring living pilot. He was the leading ace of the prestigious *Jagdstaffel* 'Boelcke'. However, the fortunes of the cocky youngster from Krefeld, and his beloved *Staffel,* were about to take an unexpected turn.

German pilots got a close look at an RFC Sopwith Pup in the wake of Werner Voss' engagement with No 54 Sqn on 9 May 1917. Pup A6174, flown by 2Lt G C T Hadrill, was chased down in a flat spin and made to force land at Lesdain, where the RFC pilot was captured. His Pup was coded 'L' on the side and had *Canada* painted on the top wing centre section (just out of view in this photograph). This was one of three victories Voss achieved that day, but they were his final successes with *Jasta* 'Boelcke'

SUMMER DOLDRUMS

On the surface, it would certainly seem that *Jasta* 'Boelcke' had done relatively well under the command of Hptm Franz Walz. In March and April 1917 the unit had compiled 36 victories for the loss of two men killed in action. However, just two pilots – Werner Voss and Otto Bernert – had accounted for 83 per cent of those 36 opponents, with the rest of the unit posting a pretty anaemic record.

Along with Boelcke, of course, many of the early victorious pilots like Kirmaier, Imelmann, König and Hans Reimann had been killed. Stalwarts such as von Richthofen, Collin, Müller and von Tutschek had been transferred to other units, where they were accomplishing great things. Then, on 1 May 1917, Bernert was also transferred out to lead *Jasta* 6. Werner Voss was the lone star performer left in the unit, and (justifiably, in terms of numbers alone) he must have felt he was carrying the whole load.

Voss' discouragement, and perhaps that of the other pilots, focused on the uninspiring leadership of Hptm Franz Walz. As noted earlier, in 1916 this Bavarian two-seater pilot had accomplished the singular feat of defeating six enemy aeroplanes while serving as leader of *Kasta* 2 of *Kagohl* I. However, as a *Jagdstaffel* commander he had failed to live up to his early promise, and had earned something of a lacklustre reputation. In three weeks as leader of *Jasta* 19 and then in five months as *Staffelführer* of the elite *Jasta* 'Boelcke' he had still not recorded a single personal victory. The writings of von Tutschek and others show that Walz did fly as *Staffel* leader, and took part in aerial combats, but he was not a successful fighter pilot who led by example as his predecessors had done.

Then, at the beginning of May 1917, Werner Voss did the unthinkable. Together with another misguided *Jasta* pilot, Ltn Rolf *Freiherr* von

Hptm Franz Walz catches a few winks in the late Spring sun at Proville. Some dissatisfied *Staffel* members might have said this was typical of his leadership style! Although it is true Walz was not an inspiring commander in the style of Boelcke and Kirmaier, there is no doubt he was an efficient and capable officer, who had scored his seventh victory on 14 May. From *Jasta* 'Boelcke', Walz went on to command Bavarian *Jasta* 34 and eventually displayed outstanding leadership of Fl Abt 304b in Palestine. This brought him his own 'Blue Max' on 9 August 1918 (*Prien Album*)

Lersner, Voss actively lobbied to have Walz replaced. A document in the files of the late historian A E Ferko bears witness to this. Voss and von Lersner apparently submitted a complaint that Hptm Walz was 'war-weary' and 'no longer fit for doing service as a *Staffelführer*' (some have opined that Voss naturally had himself in mind for the job). The written charges ended up on the desk of *Kofl* 2, the *Kommandeur der Flieger* of the 2. *Armee* (thought to be Hptm Gustav Walter), who had no sympathy for such reckless disregard for the chain of command. The complaints were given immediate attention on 18 May.

Such charges were considered extremely serious, and although Walz was judged blameless, he felt his ability to command was compromised. He requested that *Kofl* 2 transfer him to another *Jasta*. This took a few weeks to arrange, with Walz' request being met on 9 June 1917 when he moved to the command of Bavarian *Jasta* 34. He did not stay there long, for on 19 June he was transferred to his final command, Fl Abt 304b in far-off Palestine. There, Walz more than redeemed his reputation, and received a hard-earned *Pour le Mérite* on 9 August 1918 for his leadership of that unit in such a remote locale – but not for air fighting.

For Voss there were other consequences. *Kofl* 2 punished him with a 'plain' and private reprimand without witnesses, 'allowing for the extraordinary record of Ltn d R Voss, appreciating his purely objective motivation and his youth'. Voss was only saved from sterner punishment by his many victories and *Pour le Mérite*, but he had been transferred out of *Jasta* 'Boelcke' by 20 May. It was considered that the elite tradition of the 'Boelcke' *Staffel* was 'very dear' to Voss, and this transfer was a harsh punishment for him. He was transferred to *Jasta* 5, albeit as acting commander. Nonetheless, being kicked out of his cherished *Jasta* B was no doubt a bitter pill to swallow.

The location of this photograph from the Wilhelm Prien album is certainly the *Jasta* 'Boelcke' airfield at Proville, but the date and identities are more problematic. The officer reading a book at right is Hptm Franz Walz, the *Staffelführer* who left the unit on 9 June 1917. The pilot at extreme left is Fritz Kempf, then Hans Eggers, both of whom arrived in April. The man third from left has been identified as Erwin Böhme, who had been wounded on 11 February and left the unit – if this identification is indeed correct, perhaps Böhme was visiting from the *Jagdstaffelschule* at Valenciennes, as he sometimes did. At any rate, Kempf, Eggers and Walz appear to be clothed for quick take-off should they be called to 'scramble' from their folding chairs

19 May 1917 ushered in a period of misfortune for *Jasta* 'Boelcke'. That day Ltn d R Georg Noth was shot down by Ltn W M Fry of No 60 Sqn. Noth was taken prisoner and his Albatros D III 796/17 captured virtually intact. Here, the fighter's fuselage is being loaded onto a trailer at the No 60 Sqn Filescamp Farm airfield. Noth was entertained in No 60 Sqn's mess before being taken away to a PoW camp

For Rolf *Freiherr* von Lersner, there was no such leniency. He had come to *Jasta* 'Boelcke' from *Kagohl* I, and although it took two months to arrange, he was transferred to *Kagohl* 3 on 3 August 1917. There, he was killed only 22 days later.

Ironically, it was in the midst of this turmoil that Hptm Walz scored his one and only victory at *Jasta* 'Boelcke', and his first in nearly a year. On 14 May he led five other *Jasta* pilots against three DH 2s from No 32 Sqn that had been on a balloon hunt. Walz succeeded in shooting down Capt W G S Curphey, a highly experienced six-victory ace. Oddly enough, Curphey had already been shot down by *Jasta* B once before, on 4 February. He had survived a head wound at the hands of Erwin Böhme, but this time was less fortunate. Curphey's DH 2 A2622 came down and burned at Vis-en-Artois, and he died of his injuries the next day. This was Walz' seventh and, as it turned out, final victory.

With Voss gone the once crack outfit was left without any really successful and experienced fighter pilots. The resulting further decline in the unit's fortunes is reflected in the fact that not one victory was attained for the rest of May. Even as Voss was preparing to leave, the *Staffel* lost another of its pilots. Ltn d R Georg Hermann Paul Noth was no novice, having been with *Jasta* B since late January. On the morning of 19 May he crossed the lines in his Albatros D III 796/17, became lost and wound up flying alone right over No 60 Sqn's airfield at Filescamp Farm. Even worse for Noth, the Nieuport pilots were sitting in their aircraft or standing nearby when he emerged from the clouds only 1000 ft above them.

No 60 Sqn's Lt W M 'Willie' Fry, an accomplished and courageous airman with three victories already credited, told the tale in his book *Air of Battle*. He recalled that there was a great deal of excitement and pointing as the mechanics rushed to start the Nieuports. One pilot was in such a hurry he forgot to wave for his chocks to be removed and opened up his engine – his Nieuport went 'straight over on its back' as Noth's Albatros ducked back into the clouds. The others managed to take off, and Fry found the Albatros;

'By a stroke of luck, after flying around for a time, I saw it and gave chase, firing a few bursts, but I was too excited at first to take proper aim through the sight.

'It was the ambition of every young pilot to bring down a German on our side of the lines. This particular pilot, however, with me on his tail and aware that he had stirred up a hornets' nest by appearing over the aerodrome, decided to land, and did so very fast on an open space, turning over on his back.

'In the excitement of following so close on his tail, I had no idea of the height we had lost, and that we were so near the ground – I nearly flew into the top of him, pulling upward only just in time when I saw his machine tip up in front of me. I landed close by and shook hands with the pilot, who admitted that he had lost his way.'

Noth and his Albatros were transported back to No 60 Sqn's airfield. The D III's fuselage was painted green with yellow spots, and the serial number was displayed on the white tail that was now *Jasta* 'Boelcke's' unit marking. Willie Fry was credited with the fourth of his eleven victories, and the Albatros was studied by RFC technical authorities and given the number G 39. Noth was entertained in the No 60 Sqn mess and plied with drink, but he divulged no information before he was taken off to captivity.

A much worse fate befell two other pilots from the ill-fated *Jasta* 'Boelcke' on 20 May – the day Voss left the roster. Ltn d R Albert Münz had flown as an observer in Fl Abt 32 in 1916, and earned the Knight's Cross of the Württemberg Military Merit Order in August. In October he left for training at Krefeld, and he remained here until 7 April 1917, then went to a *Jastaschule* before being posted to *Jasta* 'Boelcke' on 9 May. Münz lasted only 11 days, falling in combat in Albatros D III 790/17 at Ecourt-St Quentin. *Jasta* 'Boelcke' had run into some very capable Nieuport exponents from No 29 Sqn. In the same fight Ltn d R Kurt Francke of *Jasta* B was wounded – he had been with the *Jasta* since April, but died of his wounds on 1 June. 2Lts A M Wray and A S Shepherd of No 29 Sqn were credited with victories from this combat.

With three pilots shot down in two days and its 'star turn' posted out, *Jasta* 'Boelcke' almost ceased to exist as an effective fighting unit for the rest of May 1917. Walz began the month of June with just eight pilots

According to captions in the Prien album, the pilot who pranged this Albatros D III 795/17 was Ltn Hans Eggers, who certainly seems to be posing by the tail for this obligatory photo with his hands in his pockets. Eggers came out of this crash unscathed, but two of his comrades were not so lucky on 20 May. On that day Ltn d R Münz was killed and Ltn d R Kurt Francke was fatally wounded. Werner Voss was transferred out of the *Staffel* that same day (*T Phillips*)

under his command, and of those, only Frommherz and Kempf had any victories, and not many at that. As Carl Bolle, the unit's final commander, wrote in his *Staffel* history;

'Towards the end of April and the beginning of May, *Jagdstaffel* "Boelcke" shared the lot of many good *Staffeln* – they were stripped by giving away leaders to other units and by additional losses until they were virtually completely disbanded. These many transfers amounted to virtually the same thing as disbanding the unit. For the *Staffel*, newly staffed with young pilots, an unsuccessful time arrived in their desolate hunting grounds.'

Some of the men transferred to the *Jasta* in June showed promise, including Ltn Gerhard Bassenge. Like Frommherz and Kempf, he was a Badener, having been born in Ettlingen on 18 November 1897. Bassenge had served as an infantry officer on both the Western and Eastern Fronts prior to joining the *Fliegertruppe*. He flew in *Kasta* 39 of *Kagohl* VII, a unit that was converted into *Schutzstaffel* 15 on 1 January 1917. Bassenge left that unit on 17 January and attended *Jastaschule* I. By 13 April he was flying fighters with *Jasta* 5, and on that date he attacked a 'lattice-tail' but was only credited with having forced it to land. By 21 June Bassenge was with *Jasta* 'Boelcke', where he would eventually prove a stalwart of the *Staffel*, gaining six victories – none of them were earned under Walz' lacklustre command, however.

June also saw the arrival of Ltns Franz Pernet and Otto Hunzinger, as well as Ltn d R Ernst Wendler. Pernet was born on 23 April 1895 and was the eldest son of Margarethe Ludendorff and the stepson of Gen Erich Ludendorff. He had flown in Fl Abt 14 before arriving at the 'Boelcke' *Staffel*. Little is known of Otto Hunzinger, and his stint at *Jasta* B was unspectacular. Rather more is known about 27-year-old Ernst Wendler, who was born in Ulm, in Württemberg. He first flew in *Kasta* 14 of *Kagohl* III between January and 1 July 1916, when he was wounded on the opening day of the Battle of the Somme – Wendler managed to bring his Roland C II back with a dead observer. During a lengthy period of recuperation Wendler was awarded Württemberg's Knight's Cross of the Military Merit Order. He went to *Jastaschule* I on 25 May 1917, before arriving at *Jasta* B on 7 June.

On the morning of 5 June, Ltn d R Fritz Kempf ended the three-week-long drought by downing a Sopwith Pup for his second victim. Kempf and two others attacked 'A' Flight from No 54 Sqn and 2Lt B G Chalmers came down behind German lines near Masnières. Before Chalmers was taken prisoner, he managed to burn his Pup B1729. The next day Ltn Hunzinger claimed to have brought down another No 54 Sqn Pup at 1315 hrs, but this was disputed by Ltn Hermann Becker of *Jasta* 12 – Becker won the victory arbitration and Hunzinger lost out on what turned out to be his only chance for an official *Luftsieg*. Kempf's victory on the 5th was therefore the only one confirmed for the once proud *Jasta* in the entire month of June. To be fair, most of the aerial action was up north in the 4. *Armee*, where the First Battle of Messines commenced on the 7th.

BERNERT RETURNS

Hptm Walz bid farewell to the 'Boelcke' *Staffel*, and his troubled affairs there, on 9 June. Posted back in to *Jasta* B as his replacement was a familiar

Jasta 'Boelcke', now under the command of Oblt Otto Bernert, played host to some visitors from the Austro-Hungarian *KuK Luftfahrtruppen* at Proville in June. In the top row, from left to right, are Fritz Kempf, Hermann Frommherz, Hans Eggers, Otto Hunzinger, Georg Zeumer, Karl Bodenschatz (OzbV), Gerhard Bassenge, Wilhelm Prien and Johannes Wintrath. In the middle row are *KuK* guest Hptm Hervan von Kirchberg, then Bernert, Werner Voss (apparently visiting from *Jasta* 5), *KuK* visitor Hptm Raoul Stojsavljevic and Ernst Wendler. At left in the front row is a little-known pilot usually identified as Ltn Strey (or Stren), then Rolf *Freiherr* von Lersner and Franz Pernet. Zeumer would be killed in action on 17 June. Lersner was an accomplice of Voss in his misguided attempt to have Hptm Walz removed from command, and would be transferred out of *Jasta* B in early August (*Prien Album*)

name – Ltn Fritz Otto Bernert, who had been leading *Jagdstaffel* 6. At first this news must have been greeted happily by the 'Boelcke' unit's pilots, for they knew Bernert as one of their own, a daring *Jagdflieger* who had raised his score to 27 with three tallies at *Jasta* 6. He was counted on to return aggressive leadership to the unit. However, Bernert was not a well man, and the task of restoring lustre to his old unit was plainly beyond him.

According to the book *Als Sänger-Flieger im Weltkriege* by *Jasta* 6 pilot Carl Holler, Bernert had experienced a run of ill fortune. On 19 May he had led Holler and two others in an attack on six FE 2bs from No 22 Sqn. Holler shot one down in flames and Bernert followed another one down until his engine quit. The ace managed to glide into German lines but wrecked his Albatros. A few days later Bernert was landing a replacement aeroplane when he overshot the field while landing and crashed on the eastern side of the field – his jaw was broken and he suffered severe contusions. He refused to relinquish his command of *Jasta* 6, but did no more flying there, spending some time in a sanatorium.

It is certain Bernert was still in recovery from his injuries, and was no doubt worn out, when he got the order to take over *Jasta* 'Boelcke' after Walz left. Bernert's war was one of duty, and he gamely arrived to do his best. The amount of actual combat flying Bernert did at *Jasta* B is unrecorded. It may well have been limited due to his recent injuries, combined with his near-useless left arm.

At this time *Jasta* 'Boelcke' hosted some guests from the *kaiserliche und königliche Luftfahrtruppen,* the aerial force of Germany's ally Austria-Hungary. One of these was Hptm Raoul Stojsavljevic, a prominent Austrian ace who had already racked up six of his eventual ten victories.

47

He and Hptm Hervan von Kirchberg were visiting the Western Front to become familiar with German fighter tactics and methods, and had briefly been assigned to *Jasta* 6 in late May during Bernert's time there. No doubt Bernert invited the Austro-Hungarians to visit *Jasta* 'Boelcke' as well.

As previously noted, *Jasta* B recorded only one victory in June, and on the 17th it lost two pilots. After only 12 days with the *Staffel*, Ltn d R Ernst Wendler was transferred out to take over *Jasta* 17. He was replacing Hptm Eberhard von Seel, another pilot who had served briefly in *Jasta* B before his death as *Jasta* 17's leader on 12 June. Wendler proved a capable *Staffelführer* at *Jasta* 17 before a wound in October basically ended his combat career.

The other *Jasta* B man lost on the 17th was killed. Oblt Georg Zeumer is familiar to enthusiasts of World War 1 aviation because his career crossed paths with that of Manfred von Richthofen, and he is mentioned in the Rittmeister's book *Der Rote Kampfflieger*. The 27-year-old Zeumer was already flying in Fl Abt 4 in November 1914 when he won the Saxon Knight's Cross of the Military St Henry Order. He was reported to have 'defeated' a British aeroplane with only a pistol during this period, but this did not count as an official victory. Zeumer later flew with F Fl Abt 69 on the Eastern Front, where one of his observers was von Richthofen. At the end of August both men were transferred to *BAO* in Flanders, where they continued to fly as a team.

One official report lists Zeumer as gaining a victory on 11 April 1916 when he was with *Kagohl* I, and some authorities credit him with three more prior to his arrival at *Jasta* B. The frail Zeumer had tuberculosis, and was known as 'the lunger' because of his reckless approach to flying and disregard for his own safety. He had arrived at *Jasta* B around April 1917, but had tallied no victories since. On 17 June he attacked an RE 8 from No 59 Sqn east of Honnecourt. The observer, Lt E O Houghton, trained his Lewis gun on the enemy scout and opened fire from 50 metres – the

Ltn Gerhard Bassenge arrived at *Jasta* 'Boelcke' sometime in May or early June 1917. He would not score his first confirmed claim until 20 October, but he would go on to survive the war with seven victories. Here is Bassenge's D III 2219/16, which displayed the unit's usual black-trimmed white tail and black spinner. The pilot's personal emblem consisted of the black and white perpendicular bands on the fuselage. In the distance is Kempf's D III

Albatros turned away and stalled, then went into a vertical dive and burst into flames. When he heard the news of his old friend's death, von Richthofen wrote, 'It was perhaps the best thing that could have happened to him. He knew that he had not much longer to live. Such an excellent and noble fellow. How he would have hated to drag himself toward the inevitable end.'

25-year-old Wilhelm Prien had been posted to *Jasta* B on 9 June, apparently arriving several days before Gerhard Bassenge. However, while Bassenge showed potential and would eventually emerge as a superior *Jagdflieger,* Prien failed to make much of an impression as a fighter pilot. He had been born in Hamburg on 23 December 1891, and was an engineer before the war. He followed the usual two-seater route until he arrived at *Jastaschule* I in May 1917. Pilots such as Prien, Eggers, Hunzinger and Pernet flew combat patrols in the summer of 1917 but may have lacked the hard-charging drive characteristic of successful fighter pilots. Prien would score no victories, but would last until 30 August 1917 when he was posted out.

Although June had been a disappointing month it terms of aerial victories for *Jasta* B, it is perhaps worthy of note that *Jasta* 5, the other fighter unit in the 2. *Armee,* posted five victories (three by Voss) in a flurry

Ltn d R Wilhelm Prien was posted to *Jasta* 'Boelcke' from *Armee Flug Park* 2 on 9 June 1917. At some point he seems to have taken over Kempf's Albatros D III. Prien altered the markings by adding a white disc to Kempf's original white arrow emblem. The disc and arrow were repeated on top of the fuselage (*Prien album*)

This view provides a good look at the nose of the Kempf/Prien D III and the forward portion of the arrow insignia. Note the cooling louvres cut into the cowling just aft of the spinner and the anemometer-type ASI mounted on the port interplane strut (*Prien album*)

Albatros D III 751/17 was flown by
Ltn Otto Hunzinger, another pilot
who had arrived at *Jasta* 'Boelcke'
sometime in June. Hunzinger
displayed some ingenuity in the
decoration of his Albatros, working
his *OH* initials into a black/white
band encircling the fuselage. Proudly
posing here is another *Staffel* pup,
this one named 'Prinz' *(Prien album)*

of activity during the first six days of the same month for the loss of two
pilots, then also recorded no significant activity for the next three weeks.

On 1 July *Jasta* B lost its capable OzbV (adjutant) Oblt Karl
Bodenschatz. Having received a telephone call from von Richthofen
asking him to handle similar duties for his new fighter wing,
Jagdgeschwader Nr I, Bodenschatz knew an opportunity for advancement
when he saw it and quickly accepted. His place was taken by Ltn d R
Anton Stephan. In some ways Bodenschatz was jumping a sinking – or at
least becalmed – ship. In July it became even more obvious that *Jasta*
'Boelcke' had fallen far from its glory days of Autumn 1916, for the unit
failed to record a *single* victory, or suffer a casualty, in the entire month.

According to notes compiled from the *Jasta* war diary by the German
historian Dr Gustav Bock, due to casualties and transfers out of the *Staffel*
the unit was so weakened it was pulled out of the Front for a period of rest

Another view of Ltn Hunzinger's D III
751/17, which also displayed the
unit's customary black spinner. In
the background is Frommherz' *Blaue
Maus*. Hunzinger failed to achieve
any confirmed victories, but as a
regular army officer (not in the
reserves), Hunzinger was sometimes
placed in acting command of the
Staffel during Bernert's leaves in
June and July *(Prien album)*

and rebuilding. Unfortunately, little other information has surfaced regarding this 'quiet' period, such as how long it lasted. It does help to explain the lack of reported activity by the *Jasta.*

It would seem that *Staffelführer* Bernert occasionally took some much-needed leave during June and July. Ltn Otto Hunzinger took acting command of the *Jasta* at least twice that summer, the first time on 28-29 June. Hunzinger was not a high scoring *Kanone* or a longtime veteran of the unit, but he was a regular army officer, and that counted for quite a bit. Hunzinger was certainly an active combat pilot, for as we have seen he claimed to have downed a Sopwith Pup on 6 June, but the victory was awarded to a *Jasta* 12 pilot. Hunzinger flew an Albatros D III that bore his initials cleverly worked into the fuselage décor.

On 8 July Hunzinger was again Acting *Staffelführer*, and on that date he forwarded a recommendation that Hermann Frommherz be awarded the Knight's Cross of the Military Karl Friedrich Order of the Grand Duchy of Baden. He also lodged paperwork supporting the awarding of the Baden's Order of the Zähringen Lion to Gerhard Bassenge. Medals historian Neal O'Connor described Hunzinger's actions as 'overplaying his hand', for neither of these *Jasta* B fliers had yet distinguished themselves to any great degree, and they were not awarded these decorations at this time. However, Frommherz would go on to great achievement in later months, and did receive the Order in October 1918, as well as the 'Hohenzollern'.

The only other incident of note in July was the arrival of Ltn d R Hermann Vallendor on the 5th. Like Kempf, Bassenge and Frommherz, Vallendor was a native of Baden – also like them, he would attain significant victories, but took some time to come into his own as a fighter pilot. Born in Offenburg on 13 April 1894, he rose through the ranks of the infantry during the war to be commissioned in the reserves in December 1915. In October 1916 he went to FEA 5 for pilot training and

Jasta 'Boelcke' again played host to visiting dignitaries in early June, this time a military mission of officers from neutral Sweden. The group is posed in front of Bassenge's D III, and a few *Staffel* members can be identified. From right to left, they include unknown, Hermann Frommherz, Franz Pernet, unknown, Karl Bodenschatz, unknown, then Ernst Wendler and *Staffelführer* Otto Bernert with the 'Blue Max' at his throat (*T Phillips*) flew with Fl Abt 23 in May 1917. On 24 June he left for the *Jastaschule* and qualified for his pilot's badge on 4 July.

AUGUST 1917

Whatever kind of 'rest period' the weakened *Staffel* was experiencing during July, it came to an end on 1 August when the unit was transferred north to the 6. *Armee* and set up shop at La Petrie, north of Douai. The Third Battle of Ypres had begun the previous day, putting tremendous pressure on Gen von Arnim's 4. *Armee* in Flanders. Therefore, *Jasta* B did not tarry at La Petrie, but moved north to the well-established airfield at Bisseghem in the 4. *Armee*. Between 12 and 14 August the *Staffel* relocated again, this time to Ghistelles, where it joined *Jagdgruppe 'Nord'*. The action heated up considerably, and between 8 and 14 August the *Staffel* pilots made 56 offensive patrols.

Uffz Paul Bäumer, an NCO pilot destined for a huge role in the *Jagdstaffel* 'Boelcke' saga, arrived at the unit from *Jasta* 5 in early August. He was actually making his return to *Jasta* B, as he had served for just two days with the unit at the end of June before being packed off to *Jasta* 5. Born in Duisberg on 11 May 1896, Bäumer found his passion for flying at a young age, influenced by the 'Zeppelin fever' prevalent in Germany. He worked as a dentist's assistant to pay for flying lessons, and had made several flights before the war. Once the conflict began, Bäumer served in France and Russia in *Infanterie-Regiment* Nr 70, suffering an arm wound in February 1915. After his recovery he managed to obtain a transfer to the *Fliegertruppe*, and was sent to flying school at FEA 1 in September.

By October 1916 he was posted to AFP 1, then finally back to the front as a gefreiter pilot in Fl Abt 7 in March 1917. Bäumer's reconnaissance missions in Rumpler two-seaters earned him his pilot's badge on 15 May. He also managed to fly a captured Nieuport that he had repaired, which whetted his appetite for single-seaters. Consequently, he was posted to *Jastaschule* I in June, then to *Jasta* 5. He had already burned three balloons in July at *Staffel* 5 before returning to *Jasta* B.

According to the caption in one album, this *Jasta* 'Boelcke' D III was wrecked by Ltn d R Johannes Wintrath in June 1917. Oddly enough, a different source labels it as having been pranged by Hermann Frommherz in May. It certainly seems to have been Wintrath's usual aircraft, as he is seen in the cockpit in a different shot. Wintrath had joined the *Staffel* in February. On 17 August he scored the unit's first victory in more than two months when he destroyed a Camel. Two days later he forced down another Camel, but was only credited with a 'forced to land' (*R Zankl*)

During Otto Bernert's time as commander of *Jasta* 6, Sopwith Pup B1721 was forced down and captured by one of his pilots, Vzfw Carl Holler. The No 54 Sqn pilot, Lt F W Kantel, was made a PoW on 30 May 1917 as Holler's third victory. Bernert apparently brought the Pup with him when he took command of *Jasta* 'Boelcke' (*Prien album*)

At 0815 hrs on 17 August, Ltn d R Johannes Wintrath ended the two month dry spell of *Jasta* 'Boelcke' when he downed a Sopwith Camel – the first of that vaunted type in the *Staffel* victory log. Wintrath's Camel may have been B2319 from No 70 Sqn, flown by Lt A M T Glover (who was killed), which was shot down southeast of Ypres, but there are other candidates for Glover's victor as well. Only two days later Wintrath claimed another Camel, but was only credited with an aircraft *zur Landung gezwungen* (forced to land).

Oblt Bernert appears to be all suited up for a flight in his Sopwith as a mechanic exits the cockpit. The Pup was overpainted in a dark colour overall and German national insignia then applied. Note that the scout apparently retained its Vickers gun. Bernert probably did little operational flying in the Pup

Bernert's Sopwith Pup heads a line-up of *Jasta* 'Boelcke' Albatros machines in early Summer of 1917. Next to the Pup is an early production D V with a headrest, followed by what is thought to be Wintrath's D V 1072/17, marked with blue-white-green bands on the fuselage. Next is Kempf's D III in its original finish (*Prien album*)

In the meantime, Bernert had given up command of the *Jasta* on 18 August. It was an overdue move, and certainly for the best. The weary Bernert had done some flying during his time as *Staffelführer*, but the extent of his combat operations is unknown. There are photographs showing him preparing to fly a captured Sopwith Pup, but it remains uncertain if he actually flew this machine on frontline patrols. This would not have been unusual, for there are many documented cases of Germans flying captive Allied fighters in combat. In fact Bernert's Sopwith was just one of three contemporary Pups being flown at the Front in German insignia.

On the other hand, one wonders if the Pup – famous as a delightful machine to fly – may simply have been used for personal transport by Bernert (see *Osprey Aircraft of the Aces - Sopwith Pup Aces of World War 1* for further details). This particular aeroplane had been brought down intact on 30 May by Bernert's friend Carl Holler of *Jasta* 6, and Bernert brought it with him to the 'Boelcke' *Staffel*.

Bernert was reportedly afflicted by a severe illness, and he left combat flying for good. Suffering from what the Germans called *Kriegsmüdigkeit* (war-weariness), his many injuries had also no doubt caught up with him. He was sent home to Germany. May 1918 found him at a health resort in Zoppot, near Danzig, indicating that he may have been suffering from respiratory problems too. In his weakened condition Bernert fell victim to influenza and died on 18 October 1918.

But now who would command *Jasta* 'Boelcke'? Luckily for the pilots, and reputation, of the famous unit, the right man for the job was found. The new leader was already famous in the *Staffel*, and closely associated with the great Boelcke himself – Erwin Böhme.

Oblt Fritz Otto Bernert had been placed in command of *Jasta* 'Boelcke' following Walz' departure, but he was not a well man and was hardly up to the task. He had suffered severe injuries in a crash at *Jasta* 6 and was probably still in recovery. Bernert may have done little flying during his tenure as *Staffelführer*. At any rate, he was posted out on 18 August 1917, probably due to the combined effects of injury and illness, and Erwin Böhme was brought in as the new commander (*Prien album*)

NEW COMMANDER

The last time Erwin Böhme had flown with *Jasta* 'Boelcke' was on 11 February 1917, when he received a bullet in his arm. By 8 April he had recovered enough to be assigned to *Jastaschule* I at Valenciennes as an instructor. Although this posting did not appeal to him, Böhme realised it was a 'very responsible assignment, since the quality of the reinforcements for the *Jagdstaffeln* depends thereon'. His mind was never far from the Front, however, and he kept in frequent touch with von Richthofen and the other men of his old unit.

On 2 July he joyfully received the news that he would be taking over *Jasta* 29. Böhme had worried that his age would prevent him from being considered as a *Staffelführer,* and now intended to 'show them what I am capable of doing'. He got his 13th victory on 14 July, but was lightly wounded on 10 August. As he was peppering an RFC two-seater, a British fighter surprised Böhme from below and a bullet grazed his right hand, cutting the tendon of his index finger. It curtailed his flying, but he stayed with his unit. Then, on 18 August;

'A telephone message just came through from *Kogenluft,* a complete surprise to me, that I had been assigned command of *Jagdstaffel* "Boelcke" and proceed to report immediately. I shall simply fly to my new *Staffel.* It is located not too far from here, in the surroundings of Ostende, near Ghistelles.

'The assignment is very honourable, but at first will also be difficult and require much work. Naturally, I am happy to return to my old *Staffel,* which has been sanctified through his name, even if I won't find a single one of my old companions there. And it is proof of a great trust that headquarters has handed over command of the *Staffel* to me, in order to bring it up again to its former heights. For its former brilliance has completely faded in recent times. There is nothing left of the old *Staffel* but its famous name. Now it must once again be inspired with the old Boelcke-spirit.'

Böhme found a group of mostly inexperienced pilots at *Jasta* B, and did his best to have some promising airmen transferred in. He knew there would be no lack of opposition in Flanders, with the Third Battle of Ypres in full swing in spite of the near-constant rains. The task ahead was clearly defined by his successor, Carl Bolle;

'There were two basic prerequisites for the renewed success of the *Staffel* – a theatre rich in activity, and a leader with a powerful personality. Next, there was a third task to accomplish – to form the *Staffel* into a unified fighting troop. Here is where the commander's work had to begin. The unity of the *Staffel*, and its members' performances, had both begun to wane. For that reason Böhme was summoned both to redirect this unhealthy development in the proper direction and to continue Boelcke's work along those lines. The *Staffel* had Böhme's efforts substantially to thank for its performance that continually improved right up to war's end. The *Staffel* had in Böhme a leader who was able to make its old name worthy once again.'

Ltn d R Erwin Böhme, great friend of Boelcke and one of the last surviving members of the 'old guard' of the original *Jasta* 2, was given the job of rebuilding his old unit on 18 August 1917. He wrote to his fiancée, 'And it is proof of a great trust that headquarters has handed over command of the *Staffel* to me, in order to bring it up again to its former heights'. It would prove to be no easy task

Just how formidable the enemy was in this sector was soon driven home on 22 August when Ltn Egon Könemann fell in combat with Camels near Lombardzyde. The 27-year-old was yet another inexperienced pilot who had not been with *Jasta* B much more than a month.

On 29 August Böhme reported that the *Jasta* was relocating to Varsenaere, near Bruges, since British artillery had made life in Ghistelles difficult. He also wrote that he had to again stop flying because the doctors had operated on his wounded right hand and 'a rich lead mine was discovered. My *Staffel* consists of relatively steady people and it is already becoming a going enterprise'. Although he was seeking competent new men, Böhme also weeded out those who had failed to prove themselves. Ltn d Rs Kosslick and Prien were posted to AFP 4 at the end of the month, and in early September Ltn Thiel was transferred to *Jasta* 28.

According to Böhme, the *Staffel* was now 'frequently flying over the North Sea. First, by any measure that is splendid. Second, one can now slip around quite nicely behind the other side of the front and hunt. Third, one doesn't have to be concerned about the silly flak guns over the sea. Clearly they cannot hit anything, but nevertheless they still make one uneasy.'

During one of these flights on 5 September, five Albatros fighters of the *Staffel* dived on a formation of No 48 Sqn Bristol Fighters north of Ostende, on the Belgian coast. Ltn Franz Pernet attacked Bristol F 2B A7182, flown by 2Lt K R Park and 2AM H Lindfield (New Zealander Keith Park would command RAF Fighter Command's No 11 Group in the Battle of Britain). Park's combat report stated;

'One of the enemy aircraft overshot me, and I got five bursts at very close range at it, and he fell apparently out of control, and I followed on his tail firing until a second Scout got on my tail and I was unable to watch

Ltn Franz Pernet was the stepson of Gen Ludendorff, and he had served in *Jasta* 'Boelcke' since June 1917. He flew this Albatros D III, marked with broad bands that were probably black-white-black, with a white border. Pernet was killed in action on 5 September 1917 (*A Imrie*)

Leergewicht: 675 kg.
Zulässige Belastung bei voller Tank. 135

the first enemy aircraft any longer, as the rest of the hostile formation was circling round me.'

Pernet, the stepson of Gen Ludendorff, was killed and his Albatros fell into the sea. His body washed ashore in the Netherlands several weeks later. On 22 March 1918 Ludendorff lost another stepson when Erich Pernet's LVG of Fl Abt 29 was shot down.

BETTER PILOTS

Some of the quality replacements were starting to show up. In late August Ltn d R Karl Gallwitz followed Böhme to *Jasta* B from *Jasta* 29. Born in 1895 in Sigmaringen, in the Principality of Hohenzollern, Gallwitz had served as a member of Fl Abt (A) 231 in early 1917. That summer he was assigned to Fl Abt 37 on the Eastern Front, where he destroyed two Russian balloons in July. This earned him a trip to *Jastaschule* I and then to *Jasta* 29 on 13 August.

On 7 September Ltn Maximilian Joseph von Chelius arrived. Born in Karzin on 26 June 1897, he was the second son of Generalleutnant Oskar von Chelius, formerly General in the suite of the Kaiser and now with the General-Government of Belgium. Maximilian had been commissioned in the elite *Leib-Garde-Husaren-Regiment,* a unit once commanded by his father. Ltn d R Richard Plange, born in Ellingson on Christmas Eve 1892, was posted in from AFP 4 in late August/early September. On 10 September Ltn d R Walter Lange arrived.

On 9 September *Jasta* B achieved its first victory under Böhme's command. Paul Bäumer was flying D V 4409/17, and penned the following report;

'A *Kette* of five *Staffel* aircraft took off at 1505 hrs for a combat flight to the front. Over our positions to the south of Nieuport I sighted several RE 8s, one of which was being shelled by our flak. This one I attacked at an altitude of 1000 metres, coming down steeply from above, and I caused him to fall at Vilette-Ferme. I followed the smoking aeroplane until impact. The enemy aircraft was completely smashed up and lies between the trenches. Except for the *Staffel*, no other aircraft were nearby.'

The last line is a frequent refrain in *Jagdflieger* combat reports, and is meant to ensure that no other pilot could horn in on the victory claim. Bäumer was credited with his fourth victory at the expense of No 52 Sqn – both Lt A Davidson and 2Lt B B Bishop were killed.

On 10 September Böhme was still only partially capable of combat flying because of his injured hand. He took advantage of his involuntary vacation to leave and 'raise some of the *Staffel*'s concerns directly at the source in Berlin'. He left Ltn d R Wintrath in acting command of the *Staffel*. Böhme also took the opportunity to pay his first visit in a year to his lady friend Annamarie, the recipient of his many letters. He returned on the 18th, and 'the sad news awaited me that my *Staffel* had lost Ltn von Chelius, a high-spirited comrade (Hussar Guards) who had just recently joined our unit'.

Von Chelius died on the evening of 14 September. Ironically, another general's son fell to Keith Park of No 48 Sqn, this time with observer 2Lt H Owen (see *Osprey Aircraft of the Aces 79 - Bristol F 2 Fighter Aces* for further details). Once again *Jasta* 'Boelcke' had unsuccessfully attacked a formation of Bristols from No 48 Sqn, Park reporting;

Ltn Maximilian Joseph von Chelius was a former hussar, as evidenced by his uniform. Von Chelius was posted to *Jasta* 'Boelcke' on 7 September 1917 but did not last long, falling in action only seven days later (*N Franks*)

57

Uffz Paul Bäumer was posted back to *Jasta* 'Boelcke' on 15 August 1917, coming from *Jasta* 5, where he had notched up three victories. He brought some much-needed offensive potential to the unit, and on 9 September he downed an RE 8 for his fourth success, flying D V 4409/17

'Zooming back under our patrol, I saw one Bristol circling round with an Albatros Scout attempting to get on his tail. I drove this enemy aircraft off own machine and followed, diving and spiralling on his tail until I saw its pilot fall forward in his seat. Continued firing at 25 yards range until the cockpit of the enemy aircraft burst into flames, when I zoomed up to climb under our formation. My observer watched the enemy aircraft fall in flames and crash just on our side of the lines north of Dixmude.'

The next day, 58-year-old Generalleutnant von Chelius arrived at the *Jasta* 'Boelcke' airfield to ask Ltn d R Wintrath for details of the death of his last son. His older son Victor-Wilhelm had already fallen in 1914.

Böhme scored his first victory as commander of *Jasta* 'Boelcke' with an RE 8 on 19 September, showing he had lost none of his old skill. The No 9 Sqn machine fell to earth just inside the British lines at Boesinghe, with 2Lts H Devlin and F A Wright both losing their lives.

On 20 September, the third offensive of the Ypres fighting was directed at Menin Road Ridge. Bäumer became an ace when he shot down a Camel

Uffz Paul Bäumer claimed his fourth to sixth victories in Albatros D V 4409/17, which forms the backdrop for this study of Fritz Kempf. Bäumer's combat report for 20 September 1917 describes the markings as a white edelweiss on a black background with red stripes. It can also just be seen that the aircraft displayed the usual *Jasta* 'Boelcke' white tail with a black leading edge (*A Imrie*)

flown by F S Lt Ronald Sykes of No 9 Naval Air Squadron. Bäumer was still flying D V 4409/17, marked with a white edelweiss on a black field bordered by red stripes. He recounted;

'I was flying with Ltns Wintrath and Plange. We were attacked by six enemy aircraft over the front. A Martinsyde (sic) plunged through the clouds, I followed it and shot at it from extremely close range at 1520 hrs. He fell behind the first enemy trenches and turned over.'

The wounded Ronald Sykes force-landed his Camel B3906 just inside the British lines at St Pierre Capelle, and was credited with an Albatros in this combat. He later returned to score five more times in Nos 203 and 201 Sqns (see *Osprey Aircraft of the Aces 52 - Sopwith Camel Aces of World War 1* for further details).

Jasta 'Boelcke' marked two more victories on the 21st. In the morning Böhme prevented an RE 8 from accomplishing its artillery shoot, sending it crashing down at Comines for his 15th victory. At 1750 hrs the rising star Bäumer claimed another Camel in D V 4409/17, apparently wounding 2Lt Layfield of No 70 Sqn. He wrote;

'I was flying with Ltns Wintrath, Gallwitz and Lange over the Ypres positions when two enemy aircraft appeared. One of these aeroplanes was taken by Ltn Wintrath, but he had to break off again due to a stoppage. Then I attacked the opponent. A hard *Kurvenkampf* developed. I got him well in my sights and shot him at extreme close range. Suddenly, the opponent's machine reared up and went down vertically. I followed the

Fritz Kempf is seen at left as his friend Hermann Frommherz scans the skies for any signs of the enemy. *Jasta* B was by this time largely equipped with the Albatros D V, and the pilot of the camouflaged machine in the foreground remains unknown. In the distance to the right of Frommherz can be seen what is thought to be D V 1072/17, which was flown by Ltn d R Johannes Wintrath. This machine displayed blue-white-green bands on its fuselage. Wintrath was killed in it on 25 September 1917 (*A Imrie*)

Sopwith and saw it hit near Boesinghe and burst into flames. I circled over the crash site and saw the burning machine lying there.'

These successes were offset when Richard Plange was reportedly lightly wounded and left the unit.

Like many German aces, Bäumer was a firm believer in getting to very close quarters before firing. In this he was emulating Boelcke, who once explained his technique as 'Close in and open fire! I only open fire when I can see the goggle strap on my opponent's crash helmet. That's all there is to it'. Bäumer gave the following advice to Carl Degelow;

'When you think you are close enough and have the enemy nicely in your sights, and are about to press the triggers, don't! Continue to close in, take your thumb off the trigger, raise it to your mouth, counting "One", then replace it on the trigger. Do this three times without hurrying, then fire. You are close enough then, and he must fall.'

On 23 September Böhme heard the shocking news that his friend Werner Voss had fallen. After leaving *Jasta* 'Boelcke' under a cloud, Voss had gone on to lead a nomadic career as acting commander of *Jasta* 5, then to *Jasta* 29 and 14. He was finally tapped for leadership of *Jasta* 10 in JG I by his friend von Richthofen. Voss had raised his score to 48 before falling in an epic one-sided clash with SE 5as of No 56 Sqn's 'B' Flight on the 23rd.

Another bitter blow followed on 25 September when Johannes Wintrath's Albatros D V 1072/17 was shot down in flames by Sopwith Pups of No 54 Sqn. Wintrath had been one of the most capable and trusted veterans of the *Jasta*.

OCTOBER 1917

On 27 September *Jasta* B was attached to *Jagdgruppe Ypern* and began relocating to a new base at Rumbeke – a move that was complete by 1 October. Bäumer noted that the Rumbeke aerodrome was the worst he

A mechanic assists Ltn Hans Eggers as he prepares for flight in his Albatros D V. The Albatros displays a personal coloured band on the fuselage and five-colour printed fabric on the wings. Eggers failed to score a victory in almost six months of service in *Jasta* 'Boelcke', and he was one of the mediocre pilots that Böhme had posted out of the unit in early October 1917 (*Prien album*)

flew from during the entire war, being too small and with an uneven, rocky surface. However, the accommodations were comfortable wooden barracks, and the pilots settled in. On the 5th Böhme penned another newsy epistle to his sweetheart;

'For the last few days we have been at Rumbeke in the vicinity of Roulers, not very far from the front at Ypres. Today again, the artillery barrages are stupendous. They are firing toward Roulers and beyond. Up to now our location has only been hit by a couple of stray rounds. Unfortunately, my *Staffel* has been reduced to half-strength in the last few weeks through wounds, one shot down and a big house-cleaning on my part. I miss Ltn Wintrath, who was shot down over the North Sea. Plange, unfortunately, is still on leave and is at home, harvesting potatoes. I recommended that four other members seek a career other than flying. The remainder, however, are doing well.'

The pilots posted out included Otto Hunzinger and Hans Eggers, both being sent to AFP 4 on 1 October. On the 5th Böhme dedicated the new aerodrome with a victory – a Bristol Fighter from No 20 Sqn. At this time Böhme was generally flying Albatros D V 4578/17, marked with a green band bearing the white letter 'B'. Late in the evening hours of 8 October, Uffz Reichenbach was returning from a fighter patrol and crashed from a low height onto the airfield. His D V 2098/17, displaying a black fuselage dotted in white, was destroyed and he was badly injured.

On the 9th Karl Gallwitz opened his *Jasta* B account with what the *Staffel* records call a 'Triplane', north of Zevecote. No Sopwith 'Tripes' were lost this day, and other sources simply call his victim a 'Sopwith' or even an RE 8! Although he had previously been credited with two balloons, *Staffel* records cite this as only Gallwitz' second victory. He was flying D V 4407/17 with a green band around the black fuselage.

On 10 October Böhme claimed a 'Martinsyde' which Norman Franks has identified as actually being a Nieuport 27 from No 29 Sqn RFC.

Three days later Böhme brought his tally to 18 at the expense of No 54 Sqn, which lost two pilots killed and two more captured in a large fight between their Pups and *Jagdstaffeln* B, 8 and 10 over Zarren.

On 14 October Böhme was credited with a 'Sopwith' and Gallwitz got a 'Martinsyde'. Nonetheless, it seems that Böhme had again accounted for a No 29 Sqn Nieuport 27. Gallwitz' victory is more difficult to corroborate. More verifiable is Böhme's downing of a *third* Nieuport 27 from No 29 Sqn, as the pilot landed at Rumbeke. The hapless pilot was 2Lt F J Ortweiler who, as his name indicates, was of German descent. On the 20th Böhme described his opponent for his girlfriend;

'His name is Mr Ortweiler. His family comes from Frankfurt and he is now biding his time in a German PoW camp. I recently came upon (on the 16th) an English Nieuport single-seater at the front, in which our friend was sitting. Naturally, I invited him to pay us a visit. As he did not promptly begin to descend, I became somewhat more urgent in my efforts to compel him to descend. Yet, as he continually waved at me "with his hands", I did not want to do anything to him. Then he landed safe and sound at our airfield. We laughed until we were blue in the face. Moreover, this was victory number 20.

'I am quite happy with the performance of my *Staffel* now that I have gotten rid of the duds. They are willing to follow me everywhere, and have begun to shoot down opponents. Twice this afternoon large battles between opposing fighter units occurred. In the second, over Passchendaele, my damned machine guns jammed again – just when I needed to fire. Right next to me I lost an able pilot, Ltn Lange, whom I was unable to help out of his plight. The others, however, shot down three English aircraft.'

This action on 20 October was part of a large-scale RFC raid on Rumbeke. SPADs from No 23 Sqn provided high protection for

Three comrades of *Jasta* 'Boelcke' – all from Baden – pose happily with an Albatros D V of the unit in this classic photograph. They are, from left to right, Gerhard Bassenge, Fritz Kempf and Hermann Vallendor. The Albatros was decorated with black and white stripes on the fuselage, and the *Staffel* marking of a white tailplane was modified with additional chordwise black stripes as further individual identification. Two white stripes were painted on the top wing. The usual pilot of this aircraft is unconfirmed. On 20 October 1917, Kempf and Bassenge each downed Sopwith Camels to bring the *Staffel* total to 160

bomb-carrying Camels from Nos 28 and 70 Sqns. Bassenge and Kempf were among those who tangled with No 70 Sqn, the former, in D V 2346/17 with a 'dark fuselage and black-white bands', shooting down a Camel at 1220 hrs for his first confirmed success. Kempf was flying D V 2098/17 with a yellow fuselage and white tail, and he destroyed a Camel at the same time for his third victory. No 70 Sqn lost two pilots, but *Jasta* 'Boelcke's' Walter Lange was shot down in flames near Passchendaele.

On the 24th Böhme left to represent the *Staffel* in Dessau at ceremonies marking the one-year anniversary of Boelcke's death. Gallwitz took acting command of the *Jasta*. Afterwards, Böhme took this rare chance to return via Hamburg and visit his sweetheart Annamarie on the 29th, and to propose marriage. She accepted, and later received the hesitant blessings of her parents – her father was (rightly) concerned about Böhme's chances of surviving the war.

Acting *Staffelführer* Gallwitz achieved a notable victory on the 27th. Although he claimed a 'Martinsyde' at 1210 hrs, he had in fact shot down SE 5 B31 flown by 25-victory ace Lt A P F Rhys Davids. His fellow No 56 Sqn pilots last saw Rhys Davids diving east after some German scouts. The death of this popular and accomplished pilot – the victor over Werner Voss – was a great blow to the RFC.

On 29 October Hermann Frommherz was detached from *Jasta* B and put at the disposal of FEA 5 at Hannover, and from there he was sent to the flying school at Lübeck as an instructor. He had posted two quick victories back in April, but had been scoreless since.

Böhme returned on the 30th, just as Canadian forces made the final Allied assault on Passchendaele. Rain hampered most of the flying that day, and the *Staffelführer* was occupied with catching up on paperwork. He later wrote to his fiancée, 'To my great relief, I found everything with

During October 1917 *Staffelführer* Ltn d R Erwin Böhme was recorded as having flown Albatros D V 4578/17, which had a 'natural brown fuselage and a green band with a white *B* on both sides of the fuselage'. Böhme's aircraft is seen in the background of this photo of a captured Sopwith Triplane. Unusually, this D V does not yet display the usual *Staffel* marking of a white tail. The rudder and presumably the tailplane and wings were covered with five-colour fabric

the *Staffel* to be fine. Gallwitz, who served as commander in my absence, scored one victory while I was away. He is very proud of it. He is a very young pilot, but completely reliable'.

The 31st dawned clear and sunny, and late in the afternoon Böhme got his number 21. He wrote;

'I was flying with my *Staffel* over the Front on an otherwise uneventful day. I split up from the *Staffel* on the return flight in order to visit von Richthofen, with whom I hadn't spoken in several weeks. After a coffee break I flew homeward. However, I noticed just before landing that my pilots had again headed for the Front. Thus, I also headed for the Front. High above us an English fighter squadron was swarming about. We tried to climb, as quickly as possible. Because I had used most of my fuel on my flight home, my aircraft was quite light and rose like Charlemagne. In a few moments I was high above my comrades. I climbed directly toward the English, who flew ever higher, keeping them in front of me, and constantly in my sight.

'Finally one of them had the insipid idea to come down and attack me from above. I foiled his first attack by closing rapidly with him, head on. Because of that he immediately yanked his aircraft up and was quickly about 200 metres above me again. He flew the newest type of aircraft, with a very powerful motor. From then on he made four or five unskilled attempts to attack. But each time I quickly positioned myself vertically under him so that he could not obtain a line of fire on me. At the same time he gradually began to lose height, and at an opportune moment I turned the tables on him. Now the foolish fellow lies below! The entire encounter did not last five minutes. Indeed, it certainly could not have lasted much longer, as I reached my airfield without any fuel.'

Böhme's daring, but unskilled, opponent was novice 2Lt G R Gray of No 84 Sqn, who was flying SE 5a B544. His aeroplane came down south of Zillebeke Lake and he was captured, but he soon perished from his wounds (*text continues on page 76*).

The superb SE 5a fighter was a frequent opponent of *Jasta* B from the Autumn of 1917 onward. *Jasta* 17's airfield at Wasquehal in Flanders is the setting for this photograph of two captured examples. At left are the remains of SE 5a B544 'E' of No 84 Sqn, which was shot down by Erwin Böhme for his 21st victory on 31 October 1917. The pilot, 2Lt G R Gray, was taken prisoner, but quickly died of his wounds. 2Lt A Rush of No 84 Sqn was the pilot of B566 'J'. He went missing in action on 28 October and survived as a PoW

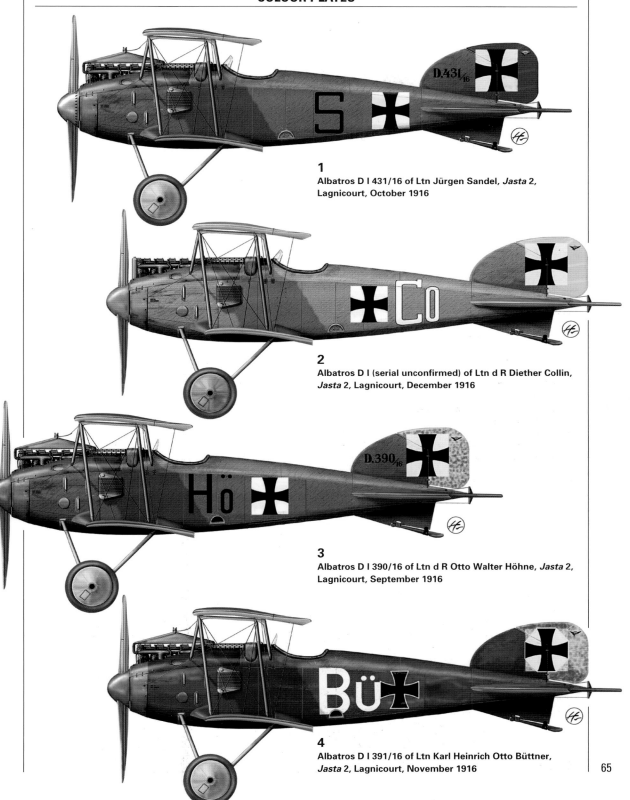

1
Albatros D I 431/16 of Ltn Jürgen Sandel, *Jasta* 2,
Lagnicourt, October 1916

2
Albatros D I (serial unconfirmed) of Ltn d R Diether Collin,
Jasta 2, Lagnicourt, December 1916

3
Albatros D I 390/16 of Ltn d R Otto Walter Höhne, *Jasta* 2,
Lagnicourt, September 1916

4
Albatros D I 391/16 of Ltn Karl Heinrich Otto Büttner,
Jasta 2, Lagnicourt, November 1916

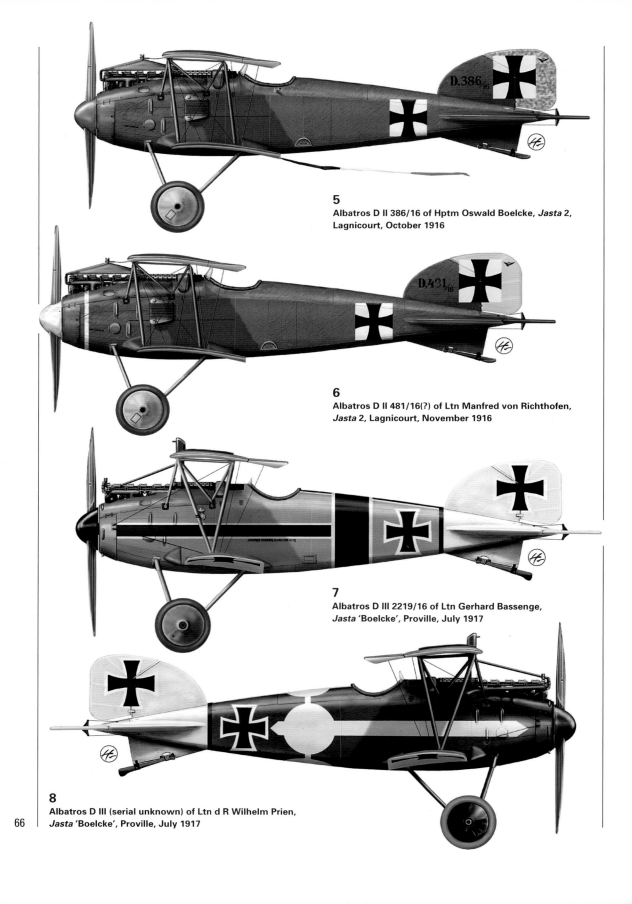

5
Albatros D II 386/16 of Hptm Oswald Boelcke, *Jasta* 2,
Lagnicourt, October 1916

6
Albatros D II 481/16(?) of Ltn Manfred von Richthofen,
Jasta 2, Lagnicourt, November 1916

7
Albatros D III 2219/16 of Ltn Gerhard Bassenge,
Jasta 'Boelcke', Proville, July 1917

8
Albatros D III (serial unknown) of Ltn d R Wilhelm Prien,
Jasta 'Boelcke', Proville, July 1917

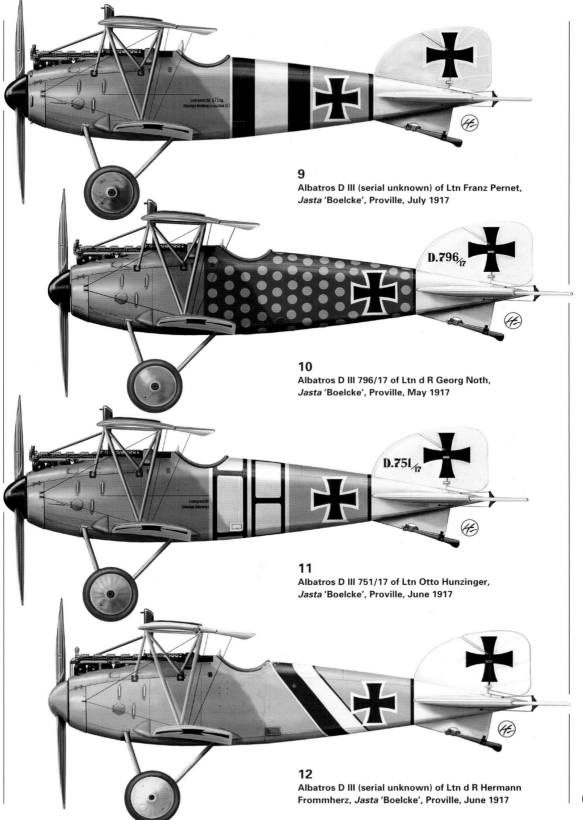

9
Albatros D III (serial unknown) of Ltn Franz Pernet,
Jasta 'Boelcke', Proville, July 1917

10
Albatros D III 796/17 of Ltn d R Georg Noth,
Jasta 'Boelcke', Proville, May 1917

11
Albatros D III 751/17 of Ltn Otto Hunzinger,
Jasta 'Boelcke', Proville, June 1917

12
Albatros D III (serial unknown) of Ltn d R Hermann
Frommherz, *Jasta* 'Boelcke', Proville, June 1917

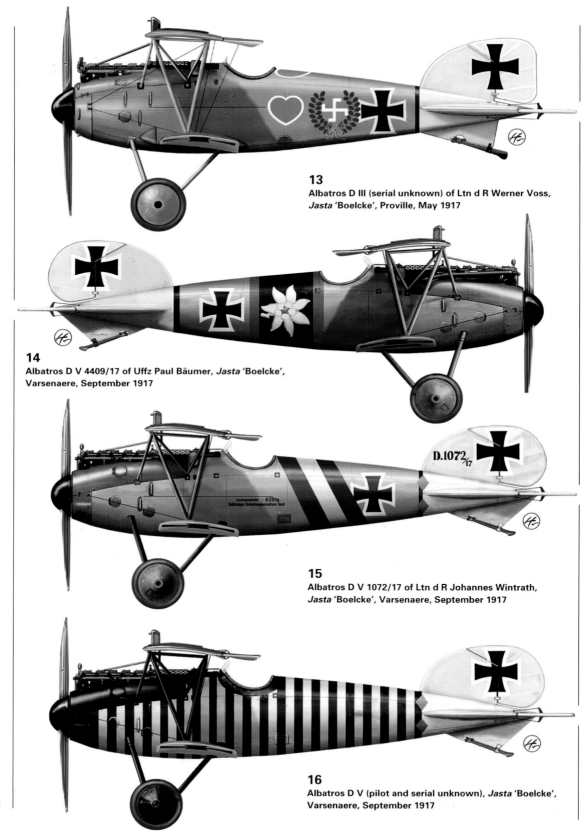

13
Albatros D III (serial unknown) of Ltn d R Werner Voss,
Jasta 'Boelcke', Proville, May 1917

14
Albatros D V 4409/17 of Uffz Paul Bäumer, *Jasta* 'Boelcke',
Varsenaere, September 1917

15
Albatros D V 1072/17 of Ltn d R Johannes Wintrath,
Jasta 'Boelcke', Varsenaere, September 1917

16
Albatros D V (pilot and serial unknown), *Jasta* 'Boelcke',
Varsenaere, September 1917

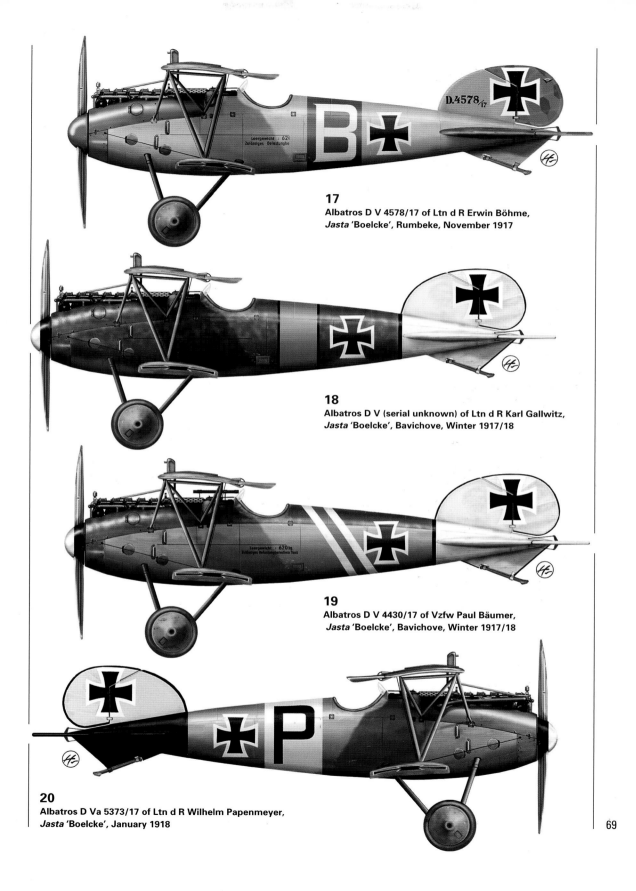

17
Albatros D V 4578/17 of Ltn d R Erwin Böhme,
Jasta **'Boelcke', Rumbeke, November 1917**

18
Albatros D V (serial unknown) of Ltn d R Karl Gallwitz,
Jasta **'Boelcke', Bavichove, Winter 1917/18**

19
Albatros D V 4430/17 of Vzfw Paul Bäumer,
Jasta **'Boelcke', Bavichove, Winter 1917/18**

20
Albatros D Va 5373/17 of Ltn d R Wilhelm Papenmeyer,
Jasta **'Boelcke', January 1918**

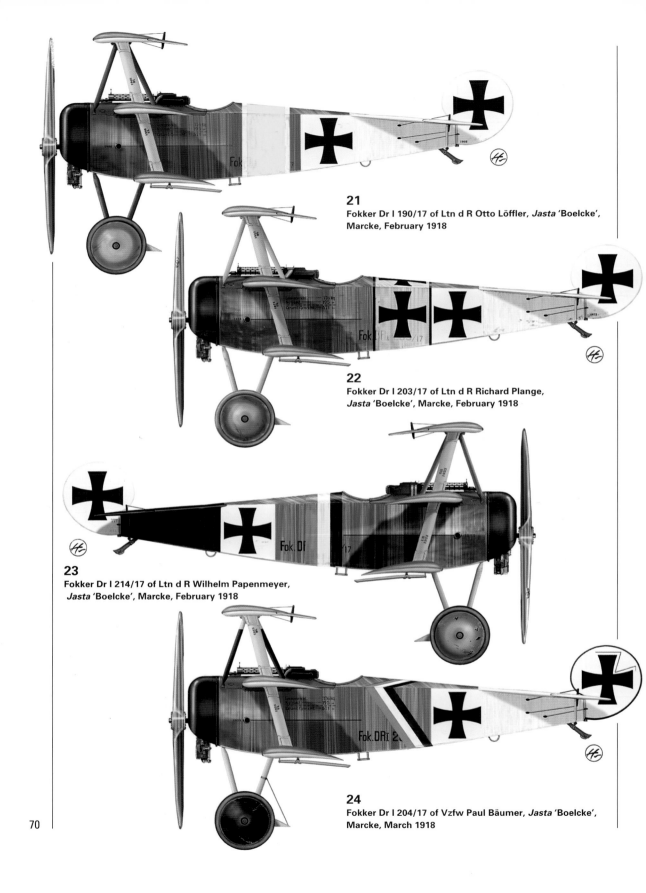

21
Fokker Dr I 190/17 of Ltn d R Otto Löffler, *Jasta* 'Boelcke',
Marcke, February 1918

22
Fokker Dr I 203/17 of Ltn d R Richard Plange,
Jasta 'Boelcke', Marcke, February 1918

23
Fokker Dr I 214/17 of Ltn d R Wilhelm Papenmeyer,
Jasta 'Boelcke', Marcke, February 1918

24
Fokker Dr I 204/17 of Vzfw Paul Bäumer, *Jasta* 'Boelcke',
Marcke, March 1918

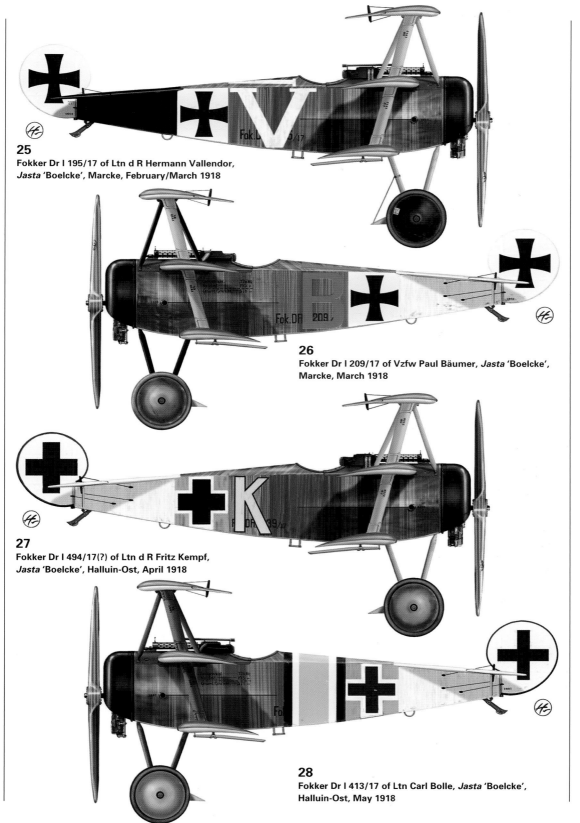

25
Fokker Dr I 195/17 of Ltn d R Hermann Vallendor,
Jasta 'Boelcke', Marcke, February/March 1918

26
Fokker Dr I 209/17 of Vzfw Paul Bäumer, *Jasta* 'Boelcke',
Marcke, March 1918

27
Fokker Dr I 494/17(?) of Ltn d R Fritz Kempf,
Jasta 'Boelcke', Halluin-Ost, April 1918

28
Fokker Dr I 413/17 of Ltn Carl Bolle, *Jasta* 'Boelcke',
Halluin-Ost, May 1918

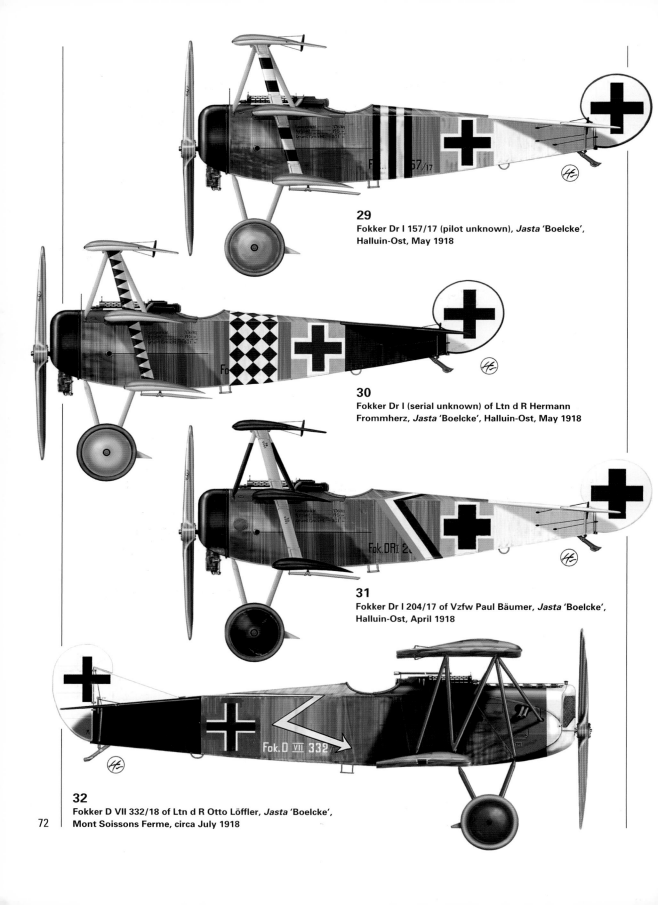

29
Fokker Dr I 157/17 (pilot unknown), *Jasta* 'Boelcke',
Halluin-Ost, May 1918

30
Fokker Dr I (serial unknown) of Ltn d R Hermann
Frommherz, *Jasta* 'Boelcke', Halluin-Ost, May 1918

31
Fokker Dr I 204/17 of Vzfw Paul Bäumer, *Jasta* 'Boelcke',
Halluin-Ost, April 1918

32
Fokker D VII 332/18 of Ltn d R Otto Löffler, *Jasta* 'Boelcke',
Mont Soissons Ferme, circa July 1918

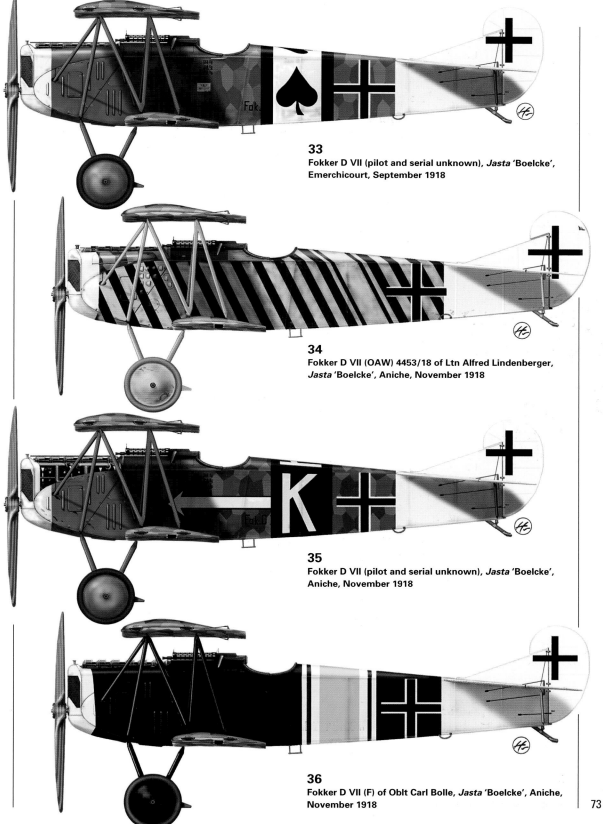

33
Fokker D VII (pilot and serial unknown), *Jasta* 'Boelcke',
Emerchicourt, September 1918

34
Fokker D VII (OAW) 4453/18 of Ltn Alfred Lindenberger,
Jasta 'Boelcke', Aniche, November 1918

35
Fokker D VII (pilot and serial unknown), *Jasta* 'Boelcke',
Aniche, November 1918

36
Fokker D VII (F) of Oblt Carl Bolle, *Jasta* 'Boelcke', Aniche,
November 1918

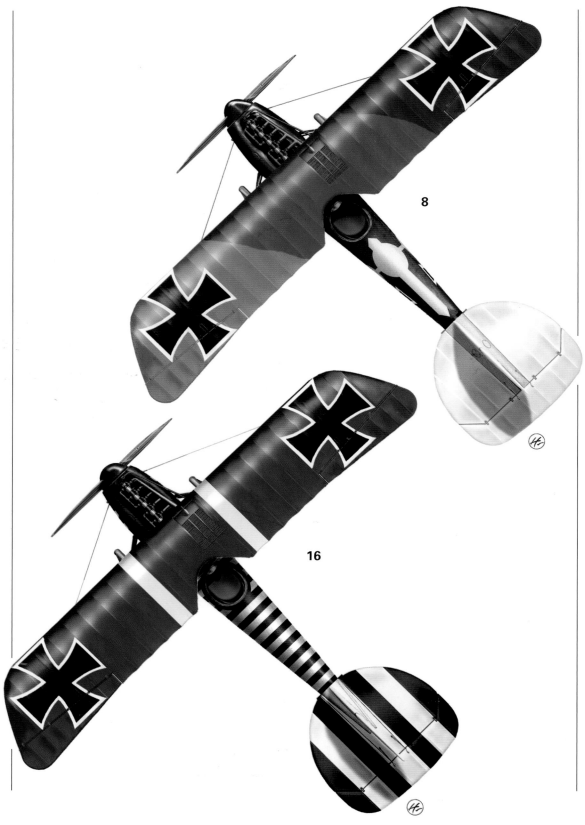

8

16

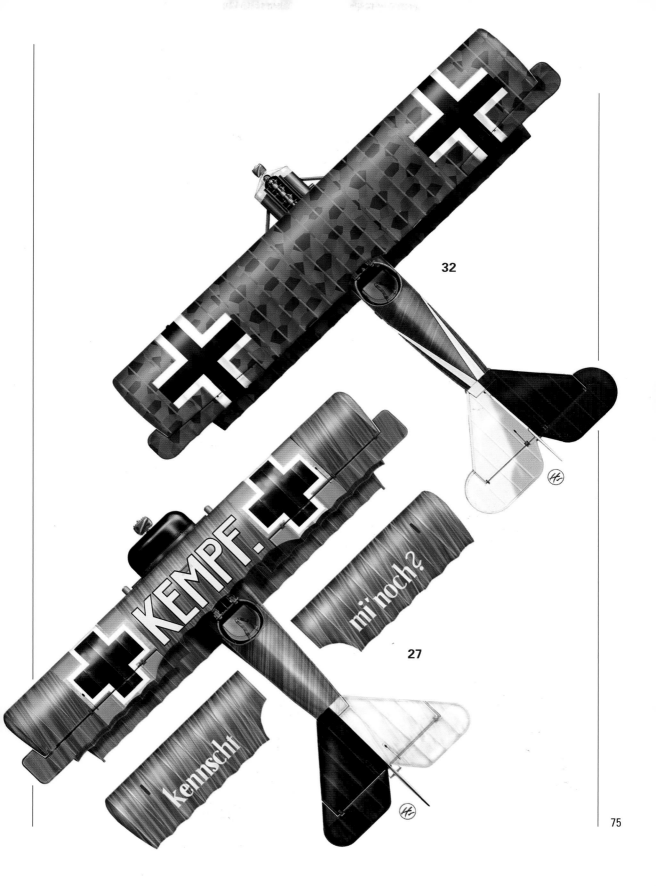

32

27

KEMPF.

mi'noch?

kennscht

This view provides another perspective on the two SE 5a trophies on the Wasquehal airfield of *Jasta* 17, with its uniquely camouflaged hangars. At this time *Jasta* 17 was part of *Jagdgruppe Ypern* along with *Jasta* 'Boelcke'. Erwin Böhme accounted for two SE 5a aircraft in October, and on the 27th Ltn d R Karl Gallwitz shot down another which was flown by celebrated No 56 Sqn ace Lt A P F Rhys Davids (*J Young*)

Ltn Max Müller transferred back to *Jasta* 'Boelcke' at the end of October 1917 from Württemberg *Jasta* 28, where this informal photo was taken. Müller was now an officer with 29 victories and the *Pour le Mérite*, and he boosted the potency of his old *Staffel* considerably

Böhme was fortunate in obtaining some very good pilots in this period. Ltn d R Otto Löffler had been transferred in from *Jastaschule* I on 19 October. He had flown in Fl Abt 7, before going to *Jasta* 19 in late October 1917. After eight months there, he went to home defence unit *Kest* 8w on 19 June 1917. On 11 October Löffler was sent to *Jastaschule* I, but only stayed a week before arriving at *Jasta* B. On 1 October Ltn Paul Schröder, a veteran of *Kasta* 30 of *Kagohl* 5, arrived from AFP 4.

Best of all, Max Müller was returning to *Jasta* B. After leaving *Jasta* 2 as an NCO with five victories in January 1917, Müller went to *Jasta* 28, where his score and his rank rose steadily. Upon achieving 26 victories, he had received the singular honour of an Active, or Regular, commission by the Bavarian Army as a leutnant in the *Flieger-Bataillon*. His 'Blue Max' was awarded on 3 September.

By October Müller was disenchanted with *Jasta* 28 due to conflicts with the new commander, Ltn d R Thuy. With his score at 29, Müller was posted back to his old unit on 3 November. Böhme was thrilled, writing, 'My *Staffel* received a very valuable reinforcement yesterday – the Bavarian Ltn Max Müller, who, with 31 victories (sic), is second amongst living aviators (behind von Richthofen)'.

MORE ACTION IN NOVEMBER

November 1917 would be an action-packed month for the *Staffel* in spite of the generally atrocious weather. On the 5th Löffler's Albatros was shot down in no-man's-land just in front of the German trenches near Passchendaele. The war diary states, 'Jumping from shell crater to shell crater, he avoided machine gun fire and joined the *Staffel* again after a three-hour march on foot'. That same day Bäumer continued his winning ways, receiving credit for a Camel south of St Julien.

6 November was a day of rotten weather – low clouds and mist – but Bäumer started things off early when he sent a SPAD VII from No 19 Sqn down at 0825 hrs just east of Zonnebeke for his eighth victory. Twenty minutes later Plange claimed his first victory with what is recorded as an SE 5a. Around 1150 hrs that same morning, a patrol of Camels from the new No 65 Sqn strayed a bit too far across the lines in the atrocious

weather, and several *Jasta* B pilots soon pounced. Böhme, Bäumer and Bassenge all claimed Sopwiths in the murky confusion. No 65 Sqn did indeed lose three pilots shot down that morning, all taken prisoner. Bassenge was also wounded just after achieving his second victory and left the *Staffel,* but he would return to claim more.

Müller downed a SPAD for his first claim since returning to *Jasta* B, although there is some confusion as to whether this was on 6 or 7 November. There was no doubt that *Jasta* B had returned to something like its old form, with its tally now around 170.

Bäumer continued adding to his bag on 7 November, flying Albatros D V 4430/17 marked with a white-red-white band on the fuselage. He found an RE 8 from No 4 Sqn firing into the German lines. 'At 0810 in the morning I saw, while flying along the Front southwest of Moorslede, an RE under me, apparently a battle flier', he wrote, indicating he believed the RFC machine was a ground-attack aircraft. 'I immediately plunged down on him and surprise attacked at a height of 200 metres, causing him to go down southwest of Moorslede. The aircraft completely crashed to pieces on the ground'.

In a postwar account, Bäumer related that the enemy airmen gallantly kept fighting to the last, and that he only pulled out of his dive just in time to zoom over the wreckage. The next day he was credited with two Sopwiths, again in D V 4430/17.

On 10 November Böhme wrote that he had been named acting commander of *Jagdgruppe Ypern,* which consisted of three *Staffeln* assembled on that sector of the Front. He was now responsible for organising the fighter patrols for all the *Staffeln* and a mountain of daily paperwork. The 11th saw Max Müller down his 31st victory shortly after noon, and a new pilot arrived from *Jastaschule* I. Ltn d R Wilhelm

On 11 November 1917 Ltn d R Wilhelm Papenmeyer was posted to the 'Boelcke' *Staffel* from *Jastaschule* I, and he made his first test flights in Albatros D V 2346/17 the next day. This photograph shows Papenmeyer in a beautifully decorated OAW-built D III, which was captioned as 'The Red Eagle' in his photo album. The fuselage has been painted with a densely mottled camouflage, in common with a few other *Jasta* 'Boelcke' Albatros machines. Oddly enough, Papenmeyer's flight log shows no sorties in an Albatros D III, only D V and Fokker Dr I aircraft. It is possible this photo was taken at the *Jastaschule* (*Papenmeyer album*)

Papenmeyer was born in Hamein on 8 December 1895. He had spent 13 days at the *Jastaschule,* making about 25 flights in such aircraft as a Halberstadt D II, Albatros D II, D III and D V. On the 12th he made two test flights in D V 2346/17, and flew on his first patrol the same day.

On 13 November Papenmeyer and the rest of the pilots flew from Rumbeke to the new aerodrome at Bavichove. Five days later Bäumer was credited with another RE 8 north of Zillebeke Lake, and Papenmeyer started off impressively with a SPAD north of Langemarck at 1100 hrs. He was in D V 2086/17, and his report reads;

'I was flying along the Front in a southerly direction with two men from my *Staffel,* and at a height of 600 metres over Langemarck met a SPAD single-seater that was chasing a German C aircraft (two-seater) hard. We immediately attacked the SPAD, which let go of the C aircraft. In the resulting dogfight, I pressured the SPAD down to about 50 metres and, following from a very close distance, caused it to crash. The aeroplane went down vertically and smashed to pieces on the ground. I observed the impact. Aircraft other than those from the *Staffel* did not participate in this air fight.'

Papenmeyer's opponent may have been 2Lt G A Cranwick of No 23 Sqn, who was killed in action. The consistently successful Bäumer claimed another RE on the 19th for his 14th confirmed victory.

The Battle of Cambrai erupted on the 20th, and the main RFC effort shifted to the south. That same day Böhme added a little variety to his victory log with a Belgian Nieuport. Five *Jasta* B fighters attacked the Nieuport from *5ème Escadrille Belge,* flown by 1st Sgt L A Robert Ciselet. Böhme's fire hit the Belgian twice in the head and three times in the heart. Robert Ciselet was one of four brothers who entered the *Aviation*

Vzfw Paul Bäumer is assisted with his flight gear by his mechanics as he prepares for a patrol. Some have identified this D V as 4430/17, but the broad white-bordered fuselage band does not seem to match the description of that aircraft's markings as much as another machine photographed with Bäumer. November 1917 was one of Bäumer's best months, in which he notched up nine confirmed victories, followed by three more in December (*A Imrie*)

Militaire – one other was killed in the war and a third was severely injured and died shortly after the armistice.

COMMAND CASUALTIES

With his score at 23, Böhme's nomination for the 'Blue Max' was already making its way through channels. The Kaiser signed the entitlement document on 24 November, and Böhme would have been immediately notified by a telegram from *Kogenluft*. The medal itself had not yet reached the *Staffel* by the morning of the 29th, when the commander dashed off a brief note to his fiancée. 'Now just a quick affectionate morning greeting! The *Staffel* is already waiting for me. This evening I will write a proper letter to you'.

That day Böhme took off more than once, and was credited with his 24th confirmed claim. Müller also recorded his number 32, but it was a fateful day for *Jasta* B. Just after 1400 hrs, Böhme and two companions were looking for trouble over Zonnebeke when they spotted a No 10 Sqn Armstrong Whitworth FK 8 on a photo-reconnaissance sortie. Böhme dived on what seemed like an easy target. The 'AW' was flown by Lt J A Pattern, with observer Lt P W Leycester, the former recalling;

'Suddenly I heard the clatter of Leycester's machine gun above the roar of the engine. I looked round to see what he was shooting at, and nearly had a heart attack. Slanting down from above, getting nicely into position 30 yards behind my tail, was an Albatros. I immediately heaved the old AW round in a split-arse turn. My sudden turn had done the trick. The Albatros overshot and suddenly appeared right in front of me.

'I sent a two-second burst of Vickers fire into him. His aircraft seemed to flutter, then slid out of sight below my starboard wing. I was pretty

Paul Bäumer paid one of his frequent visits to his old NCO comrades of *Jasta* 5 at Boistrancourt airfield on a chilly day in Autumn 1917. These men are, from left to right, Vzfw Jupp Cremer, Vzfw Fritz Rumey, Bäumer, Offz Stv Josef Mai, Vzfw Otto Könnecke and Vzfw Richard Dilcher. Bäumer's Albatros seen here was probably D V 4430/17, in which he attained at least five of his victories in November and December. His combat reports describe the aircraft as having a 'dark fuselage, underneath yellow with white-red-white band'. A diagonal band insignia can be seen just behind Bäumer's head. The white fin and rudder bore a black outline

certain that I had hit his petrol tank. Behind me, Leycester was still blazing away. When I caught sight of the Albatros again, it was burning like a torch and side-slipping toward the ground, trailing a streamer of smoke. For an instant I saw the German pilot, looking down over the side of the cockpit. Then the smoke and flames enveloped him.'

Böhme's D V fell within the British lines, and he was buried in Keerselaarhoek cemetery. The British found a document on the body that mentioned an award from the Kaiser, but they did not find the *Pour le Mérite*. The medal was in an unopened package in the mail for the *Staffelführer* at Bavichove.

There were many tributes to Böhme and his accomplishments. Von Richthofen wrote to Erwin's brother Gerhard;

'I just received the painful news of the death of your brother. In war, one becomes hard and cold. However, his death has touched me deeply – you yourself know how close a friend your brother was to me. On the last afternoon before his death, he was here visiting me at Avesnes-le-Sec, my new airfield, full of joy over the development of our dear old "Boelcke" *Staffel*, which he had led solely and single-handedly to its old heights. Now they are both united in Valhalla, your splendid brother and his great master, who of all of us was closest to him.'

Ltn Eberhard Wolff *Freiherr* von Gudenberg took acting command of the *Staffel*. He had been brought from *Jasta* 29 as the new *Jasta* B adjutant

After Erwin Böhme's death on 29 November, command of *Jasta* 'Boelcke' was soon passed to Ltn Walter von Bülow-Bothkamp. The emblem of von Bülow's 'Death's Head' Hussar Regiment can be seen on his cap – the perky pup was reportedly a *Staffel* mascot named 'Tönnes'. Von Bülow lasted less than a month at the unit before meeting his own fate on 6 January 1918

On 4 January 1918 Wilhelm Papenmeyer scored his first confirmed claim while flying Albatros D Va 5373/17. The aircraft survived until late February, but at some point was destroyed in this crash. Papenmeyer's combat report described the aircraft as having a yellow fuselage with a black *B* on a white band. The aeroplane displays the new *Staffel* marking which was instituted around the end of 1917 – the tailplane was divided into half segments of Prussian black and white. The fin and rudder remained white on both sides, but were touched off with a thin black border. This machine had painted camouflage on the top wing, but the underside of the lower wing was covered in five-colour fabric (*Papenmeyer album*)

on 20 October. The dispirited pilots had to continue their grim work, and Müller continued his own drive for recognition by despatching a DH 4 on 2 December. Three days later he scored again with an 'SE' and Löffler finally attained his first victory at the expense of 2Lt C E Ogden of No 1 Sqn, whose Nieuport 27 came down south of Houthulst Wood.

On 7 December both Bäumer and Müller successfully claimed British SPADs at 1155 hrs. On the 8th, Ltn d R Erich Daube was killed at Moorslede. He had been born in Valparaiso, Chile, on 8 November 1890 and had only recently arrived at the *Staffel*. On 9 December Ltn Theodor Cammann was posted in, already having one victory under his belt.

According to Carl Bolle, 'The search for a new leader was not easy due to the lack of qualified individuals. Only after two weeks, on 13 December, did the *Staffel* receive one in the person of Walter von Bülow-Bothkamp, who was known as a seasoned pilot in Flanders and was well known under the name "Jonny Bülow"'. The 23-year-old Ltn Walter von Bülow-Bothkamp was indeed a celebrated airman, with 28 victories and command experience.

A veteran of the *Braunschweigisches Husaren-Regiment* Nr 17, Walter was one of three famous flying brothers. Flying with F Fl Abt 22, he achieved his first two victories in October 1915. He was then transferred to F Fl Abt 300 in Palestine, where he claimed two more victories. In December 1916 von Bülow-Bothkamp joined *Jasta* 18, where he scored nine more times. He was then rewarded with the command of *Jasta* 36 in May 1917, and had brought his tally to 21 by late September, earning the *Pour le Mérite* on 8 October. His 20-year-old brother Harry followed him from *Jasta* 36, joining the roster of *Jasta* B on 2 January 1918.

Jasta B ended 1917 with a record of 189 victories, second only to *Jasta* 11 with more than 220. It fell to Wilhelm Papenmeyer to record the first tally for 1918. On 4 January he was flying Albatros D Va 5373/17, its 'yellow' varnished plywood-covered fuselage marked with a black 'B' on a white band. 'At a height of 4000 metres at about 1245 hrs over Gheluvelt, I attacked an SE from a squadron of four enemy single-seaters that was diving on our *Kette*', he reported. 'After a short attack, the opponent dived straight down. The wings broke off during the fall. German aircraft other

Another view of D Va 5373/17 provides more details of the aeroplane's markings. The damaged spinner was also divided into Prussian black and white segments in common with other D Vs of the unit at this time (*Papenmeyer album*)

The diminutive Bavarian Ltn Max Müller seems to have been given acting command of *Jasta* 'Boelcke' following von Bülow's death, but his term was tragically brief. Müller fell on 9 January 1918, only three days after his predecessor

According to one source, this wrecked *Jasta* 'Boelcke' D V was flown by Ltn d R Karl Gallwitz. If Gallwitz was indeed flying it at the time it was damaged, he was unharmed. The tail displays the new black and white *Staffel* marking. The fuselage was camouflaged with a dense mottled colour, and a personal fuselage band was also applied. Gallwitz shot down two Camels on the German side of the lines on 18 and 19 January 1918 for his fifth and sixth victories

than (those) from the *Staffel* did not participate in this air battle'. Papenmeyer's opponent was Capt F H B Selous MC of No 60 Sqn.

On 6 January Walter von Bülow, in Albatros D V 2080/17, led a flight that became embroiled in a sprawling scrap with Camels of No 70 Sqn. A patrol of SPADs from No 23 Sqn, led by Capt 'Willie' Fry (see *Osprey Aircraft of the Aces 47 - SPAD XII/XIII Aces of World War 1* for further details), came across the scene. They encountered five enemy scouts flying west, and Fry dived on one, sending a burst of 20 rounds into what he described as a black Albatros. Von Bülow's D V rolled over, and went down in a steep spiral to crash in a sodden and devastated stretch of earth east of Passchendaele, in Allied lines.

Jasta B had lost its leader for the second time in five weeks. Ltn Max Müller now led the *Staffel* in the air, and assumed acting, temporary command of the unit on the ground as well. Müller may well have felt he should be installed as permanent *Staffelführer* of the prestigious *Jasta*, and was determined to prove himself worthy.

On 9 January, Müller, in Albatros D V 5405/17, led the other pilots into the grey skies over Moorslede. At 1250 hrs they encountered an RE 8 from No 21 Sqn, with Capt G Zimmer and 2Lt H Somerville on a photography mission. In the quest for his 37th victory, Müller rashly closed to within 25 metres of the two-seater's tail, directly into 50 rounds of accurate fire from Somerville's Lewis gun. Ltn von Gudenberg later wrote a letter describing the event;

Jasta 'Boelcke' mechanics manhandle two Albatros D V fuselages down a road during the winter of 1917/18 in this interesting photograph from Wilhelm Papenmeyer's collection. The nearest aircraft displays the black and white tail section of the *Staffel* and the thin black border on the rudder and tailskid fin (*Papenmeyer album*)

'And then a few days later we lost our Max. The *Kette* together attacked an RE two-seater. The observer fired alternately upon everyone and Müller must have received a fatal hit between the first and second button of his tunic. He fell out of the aircraft because he wasn't fastened, and later on his aeroplane was completely burnt. Except for this one hit, no others could be found.'

Müller was posthumously awarded Bavaria's Knight's Cross of the Military Max-Joseph Order, giving him the title Max *Ritter* von Müller.

Wartime fliers are often a superstitious lot, and one wonders what was going through the pilots' minds as they pondered the recent deaths of three high-scoring *Staffel* leaders, all 'Blue Max' recipients. Ltn Cammann soon took acting command, and the aerial war went on as much as the weather permitted. No 65 Sqn lost Camels to Karl Gallwitz on both 18 and 19 January – according to *Jasta* records, these were his fifth and sixth victories (or sixth and seventh if both his Russian balloons are counted). The *Jasta* attained three victories on the 22nd. At 1140 hrs Plange drove a Camel down at Langemarck for his second claim. Twenty minutes later the *Jasta* mixed it up with some Bristols from No 20 Sqn, and both Gallwitz and Cammann achieved confirmed claims.

On 26 January 1917, the new *Staffelführer* was finally appointed – Ltn d R Otto Höhne, one of the last original pilots of the unit from the Autumn of 1916. After claiming five victories in those glorious days under Boelcke, he had been sidelined for nearly a year by a wound suffered in January 1917. He had only recently been appointed to lead the new *Jasta* 59, but was tapped for *Jasta* 'Boelcke' commander after a month on the job. Perhaps *Kogenluft* felt that he could bring some of the old Boelcke 'magic' to the position.

Ltn d R Otto Höhne was brought in from his new command of *Jasta* 59 to take over *Jasta* 'Boelcke' after Max Müller's death. Höhne was one of the original members of the *Jasta* from 1916, but after less than a month he was gone, as he was hardly up to the task

83

JAGDGESCHWADER III

Staffelführer Ltn d R Otto Walter Höhne no doubt gave the job his best effort, but forming a group of aggressive and competitive young pilots into a cohesive and disciplined fighting unit was a daunting task. Furthermore, the *Jasta* was undergoing some major transitions. On 1 January 1918 the first Fokker D Vs had arrived at the unit. These were to be used as trainers to provide the pilots with experience in the tricky flying and handling characteristics of rotary-engined aeroplanes, in anticipation of receiving the new Fokker Dr Is.

Four triplanes were despatched from the Fokker factory at Schwerin for AFP 4 at Ghent on 12 January, all destined for *Jasta* 'Boelcke'. Along with the triplanes, the canny salesman Anthony Fokker also sent along a group of walking sticks turned from scrap propellers as gifts for each pilot. These fashionable walking sticks became indispensable accessories for the stylish *Jasta* B pilots.

On the 14th Wilhelm Papenmeyer flew one of the first four triplanes, Dr I 203/17, from Ghent to Bavichove. He then wrote to his parents and told them how happy the *Jasta* B pilots were with their new aeroplanes. More triplanes arrived, but the Albatros D V and D Va did not completely disappear from the *Jasta* inventory for some time. Papenmeyer's flight log shows that he flew both Dr I 214/17 and D Va 5398/17 throughout February and much of March.

Since November 1917, *Jasta* 'Boelcke' had been a component of the temporary formation *Jagdgruppe* 4. Now *Jagdstaffel* 'Boelcke' was incorporated into the new *Jagdgeschwader* Nr III. Following the success of von Richthofen's JG I (see *Osprey Aviation Elite Units 16 - Richthofen's Circus: Jagdgeschwader Nr I* for further details), it was decided to form two more of these permanent groupings of four *Staffeln*.

Preparations were underway for a massive March Offensive in the direction of Amiens, and the creation of two additional *Jagdgeschwader*

The first Fokker Dr Is to be delivered to *Jasta* 'Boelcke' began arriving at Bavichove airfield in January 1918. This photograph shows a line up of *Staffel* triplanes (and one D V at extreme right) at Marcke in late February/March. Going from right to left, the first triplane is Dr I 195/17, displaying the white *V* emblem of Hermann Vallendor on its fuselage and upper wing, then Dr I 203/17, flown by Richard Plange, which had an additional Iron Cross insignia on an off-white band, then Otto Löffler's Dr I 190/17, marked with his white-bordered yellow band, and finally Paul Bäumer's famous Dr I 204/17, with its tricolour fuselage band. The remaining triplanes cannot be identified with any accuracy. All the aircraft display the *Jasta* 'Boelcke' black and white colours on their tails

Ltn d R Otto Löffler forced down a DH 4 on 3 February 1918 for his second confirmed victory. Löffler's Dr I 190/17 was marked with a white-bordered fuselage band which was likely in the lemon yellow colour of his old unit, *Grenadier-Regiment König Wilhelm II Nr 10*. The aeroplane also displayed the black and white cowling which characterised most *Staffel* triplanes (*A Imrie*)

would permit each of the three attacking armies to have one of these fighter wings as part of its aerial forces. So, on 2 February 1918, Royal Prussian *Jagdgeschwader* Nr III was formed in the 4. *Armee*, consisting of *Jagdstaffeln* 'Boelcke', 26, 27 and 36. *Jagdgeschwader* Nr III would be commanded by Hptm Bruno Loerzer, who would lead it until the armistice. Loerzer had 22 victories by this time, and had long commanded *Jasta* 26. In early February *Jagdstaffeln* 26 and 27 shared Bavichove airfield with the 'Boelcke' *Staffel*, and pilots from those units practised rotary engine conversion with the Fokker D Vs that had been used by *Jasta* B.

As JG III was in the process of getting organised, fighter patrols continued, weather permitting. On 3 February Otto Löffler shot up DH 4 A7873 from No 25 Sqn for his second victory. The de Havilland, flown by Lt E G Green, with Lt P C Campbell-Martin as observer, was on its way to bomb the railway sidings at Melle when six *Jasta* 'Boelcke' triplanes attacked at about 1040 hrs. Surrounded, Green dropped his bombs and made a run for the lines, but Löffler's deadly bursts fractured his hip, then cut his petrol pipes and tail control cables. Losing fuel, he brought the DH 4 down in a forced landing southeast of Mariakerke, near Ghent, where he and his observer were captured.

Later that same day, Paul Schröder was credited with a 'Sopwith biplane' east of Moorslede and Hermann Vallendor claimed an SE at the same location and time. These were the first victories for both pilots. As noted, there were still Albatros fighters in use, for on this day Ltn d R Erwin Klumpp was killed in the crash of D Va 5420/17 at Thielt – he had been with the *Staffel* less than a month.

Ltn Carl Bolle was the final commander of *Jasta* 'Boelcke', and one of the best. Transferring from Württemberg *Jasta* 28 on 20 February 1918, Bolle began reviving the fortunes of the famous *Staffel*, and the unit entered a new and successful era

This photograph seems to have recorded the friendly transfer of command of the *Staffel* from Ltn d R Höhne to the newly arrived Ltn Carl Bolle. Several of the pilots in front of the Dr I hangar show off their walking sticks turned from scrap propellers, given to them as gifts from Anthony Fokker. These men are, from left to right, Karl Gallwitz, Richard Plange, Fritz Kempf, Harry von Bülow, Paul Schröder, Bolle, Höhne, Wilhelm Papenmeyer, Hermann Vallendor, Otto Löffler and Paul Bäumer (*Papenmeyer album*)

By mid-February Ltn d R Höhne apparently realised that he was simply in over his head, and he was not up to the task of leading a crack *Jasta* within an elite *Jagdgeschwader*, especially with the great offensive approaching. According to Carl Bolle, Höhne 'gave the leadership up again after a short period because he felt he was not mature enough for the requirements'.

On 20 February the command was agreeably handed over to Ltn d R Bolle, who transferred in from Württemberg *Jasta* 28. As Bolle himself said, *Kogenluft* was taking a gamble in choosing him – it was his first command, and he currently had only five victories after flying in Flanders for about a year. Yet it turned out to be an extremely astute decision. He would serve out the rest of the war as *Jasta* 'Boelcke' commander, perhaps the best leader since Boelcke himself.

Bolle was a true Berliner, born on 20 June 1893. His grandfather was a famous businessman who had made his name as a supplier of milk to all of Berlin. Young Carl (also spelled Karl) grew up on a large estate surrounded by horses and became an avid athlete, participating in sports such as ice hockey and rowing. After his early education, he attended Oxford University, and obviously spoke English well. Returning to Germany, in October 1913 Bolle enlisted as a one-year volunteer in the *Kurassier-Regiment von Seydlitz (Magdeburgisches)* Nr 7. He went to war with this unit and served on both Western and Eastern Fronts, but eventually he transferred to aviation like so many other underused cavalrymen.

Bolle initiated his flight training in early 1916 at Johannisthal, then went to FEA 5 in Hannover. In July he was given the choice assignment of serving in *Kagohl* IV. In October 1916 his aircraft was attacked by five French fighters, and although wounded, Bolle managed to bring his aeroplane down just inside friendly lines and drag his injured observer to safety as enemy shellfire began to fall on their machine. After recovery, he was posted to *Jasta* 28 in Flanders in April 1917. There, he came under the skilful tutelage of Offz Stv Max Müller, and Bolle would credit much of his success to the Bavarian's advice. On 18 August 1917 Bolle claimed his first confirmed *Luftsieg*, followed by four more before he was given the challenge of leading *Jasta* 'Boelcke'.

The day after Bolle took over, Hptm Loerzer assumed command of JG III, which could then be considered operational. By then *Jasta* B had moved to Marcke, near Courtrai. *Jagdstaffeln* 26 and 27 were at nearby Marckebeeke and *Jasta* 36 was at Kuerne. As Bolle wrote, the *Jasta* had 'a quiet period for a certain span of time. The transfer to the staging areas for the "Great Battle" in France that followed shortly afterwards, and the corresponding scaling back of aerial activities, provided the leader and the *Staffel* with the leisure to get to know one another.'

The next successful combat in this 'quiet period' did not take place until 24 February, when Papenmeyer scored his third victory, but his first while flying his Dr I 214/17. At 1545 hrs he stalked an RE 8 from No 4 Sqn, and reported 'at a height of 1200 metres, I attacked an RE two-seater flying in the direction of Poelkapelle. After a short dogfight, the observer sank down in his seat. The aircraft went into a nosedive. Motor had stopped running. I followed him down to about 100 metres above the ground and saw him crash into shell craters to the south of St Julien'.

Only two days later Richard Plange destroyed a SPAD VII from No 19 Sqn at 1010 hrs, apparently also while flying his triplane. 2Lt J L McLintock was killed when his SPAD VII B6871 was shot down near

Wilhelm Papenmeyer destroyed an RE 8 on 24 February for his third victory while flying this Dr I 214/17. The fuselage was marked with bands in the German national colours of black-white-red. The light-coloured rectangle on the black section of the tailplane suggests that, like Bäumer's 204/17, this Dr I may have once been marked with an additional Iron Cross on the tailplane (*Papenmeyer album*)

On 26 February Ltn d R Richard Plange notched up his own third victory, perhaps while flying this Dr I 203/17. Plange's triplane displayed supplementary national insignia on a pale-coloured band just in front of the normal Iron Crosses. Plange would achieve his number four on 26 March, after the start of the great Spring Offensive

Comines. Josef Jacobs of *Jasta* 7 also claimed this SPAD, but Plange received the credit and thus had his third confirmed victory.

LITTLE ACTION

Things were indeed quiet in early March as Germany was conserving its aeroplanes, fuel and other supplies for the coming Offensive. On the 9th Vzfw Paul Bäumer successfully claimed a Camel at 1110 hrs north of Zonnebeke, while flying his famous Dr I 204/17. That morning five triplanes from *Jasta* B took off and flew past Menin toward Ypres. Baumer wrote;

'I was flying with four other men from the *Staffel* to the Wytschaete Bend, when we saw three single-seater flights of seven aircraft each flying in formation to our front. We attacked the lower flight at a height of 2000 metres over Becelaere. First I had a *Kurvenkampf* (banking fight) with a Sopwith that I had to break off from again. Then I followed three Sopwith single-seaters from the same flight which were flying together. At a height of 1500 metres I attacked one of these, whereupon he flew towards me. After a short banking fight, I, from close range, caused the Sopwith to crash. The Sopwith reared up and then dived down vertically. I followed the falling opponent and saw him run vertically into the ground north of the Zonnebeke-Frezenberg road. The aircraft was completely destroyed.'

His fellow *Jasta* 'Boelcke' pilot Otto Löffler confirmed Bäumer's victory. It appears *Jasta* B and *Jasta* 36 tangled with Camels from No 65 Sqn, who nonetheless did not lose anyone this day.

Paul Bäumer and the Fokker triplane were a perfect fit, and he loved his new fighter. Triplane ace Josef Jacobs of nearby *Jasta* 7 had this to say about Bäumer (see *Osprey Aircraft of the Aces 40 - Fokker Dr I of World War 1* for further details);

'There were basically two groups of fighter pilots – one group preferred aircraft with in-line engines as in the Albatros and the Fokker D VII, while the second group of pilots had a preference for fighters with rotary engines. Both Bäumer and I preferred the rotary engine, and so it is not surprising that he was thrilled about flying the Fokker Dr I.'

It will be noted that Bäumer's Dr I 204/17 had a large Iron Cross insignia painted on the horizontal stabiliser, along with most of the triplanes in *Jasta* 36 and possibly (initially) Papenmeyer's Dr I 214/17. It would seem that other German pilots had mistakenly attacked some of the

triplanes in the 4. *Armee,* and these additional markings were an attempt to improve their recognition. Josef Jacobs later explained;

'As the Fokker Dr I came into service over the Front, they were often thought to be British Sopwith Triplanes by inexperienced German pilots who often "had a go" at a Fokker Dr I in the heat of battle. The most critical time was in the late afternoon and early evening, when the surface of the upper wings and the fuselage strongly reflected the light, making it nearly impossible to distinguish the national markings.'

In any case, most of the national insignia on the tailplanes were over-painted when the *Jasta* 'Boelcke' unit markings were applied. Since the beginning of 1918, the old unit insignia of white tails had been changed to half white/half black tails, with the centre line of the fuselage being the demarcation point. The new black and white colours of the *Jasta* were also applied to the cowlings in a distinctive style. This permitted the aircraft of *Jasta* 'Boelcke' to be identified from any angle, especially in large

In the foreground is Papenmeyer's first Dr I 214/17, while Kempf's famous Dr I 213/17 is in the rear. Kempf was a *Kette* leader, and his triplane was fitted with streamers at each lower wingtip. 213/17 also displayed Kempf's name in bold white letters on the top wing. To quote Alex Imrie, 'His *KENNSCHT MI NOCH?* (Remember me still?) is in the *"alemannisch"* dialect of his native Freiburg' (*Papenmeyer album*)

Vzfw Bäumer flew this Dr I 204/17, photographed at Marcke. Additional national insignia were painted on thinly applied white panels on both bottom wing uppersurfaces, and also on the centre of the tailplane. The black-outlined rudder was a common, but not universal, feature of *Jasta* 'Boelcke' triplanes. The pilot's main individual marking consisted of the red-white-black band on the fuselage. Bäumer tallied his 19th victory with a 'Sopwith' downed on 9 March 1918 (*A Imrie*)

Fritz Kempf was an old hand and a highly decorated *Kette* leader within the *Staffel* at this time (a *Kette* was a flight of three to six aircraft). His triplane's flamboyant markings are evidence of his confidence and his standing within the unit. He would survive the war with four victories (*Papenmeyer album*)

Jagdgeschwader formations. For similar reasons, each of the *Staffeln* in JG III were identified by coloured cowlings (along with other markings) – *Jasta* 26 used black cowlings with black and white banded fuselages, *Jasta* 27 had yellow noses and tails and *Jasta* 36 used blue noses.

Of course, in addition each *Jasta* 'Boelcke' pilot devised a personal marking which was generally displayed on the fuselage aft of the cockpit, although considerable latitude was allowed in the application of these insignia. Both Papenmeyer and Bäumer used variations of the German national black-white-red colours, while other pilots used markings derived from their old regimental colours. As an experienced pilot and *Kette* leader, Ltn d R 'Fritz' Kempf had leader's streamers trailing from the wingtips of his Dr I, along with *KEMPF* in large letters on the top wing and his famous *kennscht mi noch?* legend emblazoned on the middle wing.

On 12 March the *Jasta* pilots were all called to the office of Ltn Bolle, who told them that the *Jagdgeschwader* was being transferred south to the 17. *Armee*. Naturally, the rumours and speculation began, as all the personnel knew that the big offensive was in the offing. However, before they left Marcke, the RFC paid them one last farewell visit on the 13th. British bombers raided a number of airfields that day and *Jasta* B was hit hard. Six aircraft were destroyed, among them Wilhelm Papenmeyer's

On 13 March 1918 there was a deadly RFC bombing raid on the *Staffel* aerodrome at Marcke, killing five ground personnel and wounding eleven more. Six aircraft were destroyed, among them Papenmeyer's Dr I 214/17 which was written off due to the damage evident in this photograph (*Papenmeyer album*)

Dr I 214/17. Eleven men were wounded (one of them was one of Bäumer's mechanics, Monteur Stahlmann) and five groundcrewmen were killed. The five dead mechanics were Uffz August Schmidt, Gefr Ferdinand Niemann and Flgrs Vinzent Starzynsky, Georg Kabus and Arnold Nieraad.

On the 15th *Jasta* 'Boelcke' and the rest of the JG III *Staffeln* transferred to Erchin, some ten kilometres southeast of Douai, in the 17. *Armee* in preparation for the coming offensive. The *Geschwader* aircraft would operate from a spacious expanse of flat farmland east of Erchin village. In order to keep this large concentration of aeroplanes a secret from prying RFC observation aircraft, the *Geschwader* machines were dispersed and hidden in farm buildings throughout the area. No hangar tents were pitched at the airfield, and pilots were restricted to just a few flights in order to familiarise themselves with the area – they were forbidden from engaging in air fights. Hangar tents would not be pitched until the evening of 21 March, after the offensive had started.

KAISERSCHLACHT

Germany's final great gamble to win the war began at 0445 hrs on 21 March 1918. On a 70-kilometre-wide front, in the sectors of the German 17., 2. and 18. *Armeen,* a massive bombardment from some 10,000 artillery pieces shook the earth. The whole front was covered in fog, and at about 0940 hrs German assault troops went over the top behind a creeping barrage against the British Third and Fourth Armies. The Imperial Battle, or *Kaiserschlacht,* had begun.

In the 17. *Armee,* the heavy fog and low clouds that aided the ground troops prevented aerial action until about midday. The heavy

Every pilot was dependent on his groundcrew, and here Bäumer poses with his trusted mechanics in front of Dr I 204/17. They are, from left to right, Uffzs Henke and Bäumer and Gefr Meissner and Monteur Stahlmann. Historian Alex Imrie suggests that this triplane's Nieuport-type propeller indicates the Dr I was likely powered by a captured Le Rhône engine. At the time this photograph was taken, the painting of the cowling in *Staffel* colours was not yet complete (*A Imrie*)

concentration of *Jagdstaffel* aircraft ensured aerial supremacy, allowing the army cooperation machines to fulfill their missions. *Jasta* 'Boelcke' made no claims on the 21st, but on the afternoon of the 22nd, the aircraft of JG III were engaged in a large-scale battle with RFC squadrons over Cambrai. *Jasta* 26 made two claims but *Jasta* B remained scoreless.

During the afternoon of 23 March, Bäumer was flying his Albatros D V on a *Staffel* patrol. He became separated from the rest of his unit and joined up with a group of *Jasta* 36 aircraft. At a height of 2000 metres, south of St Leger, the group attacked a flight of Camels from No 46 Sqn. Bäumer got behind one and achieved his 20th confirmed claim.

At 1500 hrs that same day the Fokker triplanes of *Jasta* B took off, but Bäumer was grounded for 15 minutes with engine problems. Finally airborne, he flew west toward Arras;

'In the fog below me I sighted an enemy reconnaissance aeroplane (RE) flying at a height of 800 metres. Coming out of the sun, I positioned myself under his tailplane. The enemy gave me little chance of shooting and tried to escape, heading for Arras. I remained behind him and finally managed to approach him and so shot him down. The aircraft's left wing hit the ground, causing it to crash. It was completely smashed up.'

Bäumer was hardly done for the day. After being shelled by his own flak, he headed southeast toward Bapaume in search of his *Staffel* mates. Flying alone did not bother him – in fact he was one of those lone hunters who preferred it that way. At 1615 hrs he spotted another RFC two-seater;

'I sighted a second RE and attacked it at a height of 1000 metres. After seeing me, he turned and attacked, shooting all the time. I dived down and passed under him, turned and came up on his tail. After a short burst, he went down in flames. Pieces of the wreck fell north of Beugnatre, still burning. No other German aircraft participated in the fight.'

Equipped with the latest fighter design Germany could offer, and now commanded by a capable and inspiring leader, the pilots of *Jasta* 'Boelcke' display a distinct sense of style, confidence and *panache* in this wonderful photograph, taken in February or March 1918. They are, from left to right in the front row, Vallendor, Schröder, Bolle, Plange, and Papenmeyer. In the back row, from left to right, are Löffler, Kempf, Harry von Bülow, Gallwitz and Bäumer. Once again Fokker's prized walking sticks are in evidence (*Papenmeyer album*)

Three days later, as German ground forces advanced, the wreckage of what was believed to be one of Bäumer's RE 8 victims from 23 March was discovered near Beugnatre. Carl Bolle reported that, 'The following hits were found on the wreckage – one MG (machine gun) hit in the engine cowling, three MG hits in the outer part of the propeller blade, three MG hits in the undercarriage and two MG hits in the petrol tank (ricochets). The fuselage has been completely destroyed by fire.'

A few days later Bäumer received a telegram from *Kogenluft* von Hoeppner congratulating him on his three victories on the 23rd, which brought his total to 22. He had already received the *Goldene Militär Verdienstkreuz* or Military Merit Cross in Gold, (the highest Prussian bravery award for an NCO) on 12 February 1918.

As the offensive progressed, with great gains on the ground, the aerial combat continued with its own unrelenting severity. On 26 March Richard Plange shot down a Sopwith Dolphin from No 19 Sqn over Grévillers Wood at 1715 hrs (see *Osprey Aircraft of the Aces 48 - Sopwith Dolphin and Snipe Aces of World War 1* for further details). The type being fairly new, he called it a Martinsyde, but he was clearly hitting his stride with his fourth victory. In the *Staffel* war diary, this victory is counted as the unit's 200th. Modern historians may disagree with this depending on the criteria and numbering system in use, but at some point in March there was certainly a celebration at the *Jasta*.

The fighting continued unabated on the 27th. At 1100 hrs Gallwitz shot down Bristol F 2B B1156 of No 20 Sqn south of Albert. Capts K R Kirkham MC and J H Hedley were both taken prisoner. In the evening Plange successfully claimed an RE 8 southwest of Albert, and then he and Hermann Vallendor both despatched SE 5a fighters in the same vicinity. They had fought with No 56 Sqn, which lost Lt W S Maxwell killed when his SE B119 went down in flames. Capt Cyril Crowe, a formidable SE ace of No 56 Sqn, described this fight with the skilful pilots of *Jasta* 'Boelcke';

'I suddenly heard a machine gun behind me and discovered an enemy triplane on my tail. This was about at 1815 hrs. I immediately did a left hand climbing turn and had a most interesting scrap at 4000 ft that lasted about four minutes. The triplane could turn quicker than my 200 hp SE,

As a replacement for his triplane destroyed by the bombing raid on Marcke, Papenmeyer acquired this Dr I 409/17. He first flew this aeroplane from the new *Staffel* airfield at Erchin on the opening day of the great offensive, and alternated between it and Albatros D V 5398/17 for the next week. On 28 March 1918 he was killed while flying this triplane (*Papenmeyer album*)

In mid-April 1918 JG III was transferred to Halluin-Ost aerodrome in the 4. *Armee* sector, where this photograph was taken. The triplanes now display the initial style of thick cross bars in their new *Balkenkreuz* insignia. First in line is another of Fritz Kempf's machines, probably 493/17 which he used to gain his fourth victory on 8 May. It bore white wing markings almost identical to those seen on his earlier 213/17, but the *K* on the fuselage is now a different colour outlined in black. Third in line is Bolle's Dr I 413/17. Note that the first two machines have the pattern of black/white tail marking reversed to the others, possibly as a form of *Kette* identification (*A Imrie*)

which manoeuvre he used considerably, but my SE invariably managed to keep above him. It was impossible to keep sights on the triplane for more than a few seconds. Eventually the triplane dived east all out. I chased him as far as Contalmaison down to about 1000 ft and then left him.'

On 28 March Wilhelm Papenmeyer got his fourth victory, but failed to return from the flight – a bitter blow for the *Jasta*. At about 1020 hrs he latched onto a two-seater, flying his second Dr I 409/17. The RFC reconnaissance aeroplane was probably an RE 8 from No 5 Sqn, which lost 2Lt P W Woodhouse and Lt S Collier MC killed in action. *Jasta* records state that Papenmeyer shot down the RE near Thelus-Bailleul, and that the two-seater broke up in the air. However, it seems that the RFC observer got in a lethal burst at Papenmeyer's triplane before he died. Dr I 409/17 came down near Acheville.

As German forces advanced, the OzbV Ltn von Gudenberg was sent out to locate Papenmeyer's body. According to von Gudenberg's findings, Papenmeyer was wounded, but he managed to get his Dr I down into no-man's land just beyond the German frontlines. He got out of the triplane and crawled to a shell crater or trench, where he bled to death – his body was found by German infantry a couple of days later. Papenmeyer had a brother named Fritz who was also in the air service. The *Jasta* B leaders made efforts to have him transferred to their *Staffel* but it would take some time.

The advance ceased on the day Papenmeyer died, and victories eluded the pilots of *Jasta* 'Boelcke' for several weeks. On 1 April the new independent RAF was formed by merging the RFC with the RNAS, but that mattered little to the airmen of *Jasta* 'Boelcke'. On 10 April Paul Bäumer was commissioned as a leutnant in the reserves. With his score at 22, his new officer status would have allowed his name to be put forward for the *Pour le Mérite,* but that prestigious award would be considerably delayed. Two days later, on the 12th, JG III was transferred north to the 4. *Armee* for the coming Kemmel Offensive. The *Geschwader* occupied the aerodrome at Halluin-Ost, about ten kilometres south of Courtrai.

On 21 April (a date fraught with significance for World War 1 air enthusiasts) Gallwitz claimed a Camel west of Bailleul. It is just possible his opponent was the celebrated Australian ace Capt R A 'Bob' Little of No 203 Sqn, who was forced to land west of Bailleul within the British lines. This was Gallwitz' final victory of the war, and is counted as either his ninth or tenth, depending on the source.

However, this success paled against the news that Rittmeister Manfred von Richthofen, the most celebrated alumnus of *Jagdstaffel* 2/'Boelcke', had failed to return from a flight over the Somme. After doubling his master Boelcke's score with 80 confirmed claims, von Richthofen was shot down by ground fire at Morlancourt Ridge, on the 2. *Armee* front.

On 25 April the German attack on Kemmel Ridge began, and as German storm troops moved forward, they were assisted by low-flying Halberstadt and Hannover two-seaters of 16 *Schlachtstaffeln* (battle squadrons, formed as ground-attack units). The two-seaters were under the protection of fighters from ten *Staffeln*, assembled in two *Jagdgruppen*, while the triplanes and other aircraft from JG III gained supremacy in the higher airspace. In this fighting Bolle gained his first victory with *Jasta*

Although taken some weeks earlier, this photograph shows most of the *Jasta* Boelcke pilots who were on hand on the first day of *Kaiserschlacht*. The exception is Harry von Bülow, who transferred to *Jasta* 36 on 11 March 1918. They are. from left to right, Papenmeyer, Löffler, Gallwitz, Vallendor, Bolle, Kempf, Harry von Bülow, Plange, Schröder and Bäumer. At Bolle's feet is the *Staffel* mascot 'Tönnes' (*Papenmeyer album*)

'Boelcke' when he downed a No 73 Sqn Sopwith Camel southeast of Wulverghem for his sixth kill.

Four days later Plange brought his own score to seven with a 'SPAD' near Westoutre. This may have been a French aircraft from *Escadrille* SPA68. That same day, however, Ltn d R Ludwig Vortmann of *Jasta* 'Boelcke' was killed in a duel with SEs from No 74 Sqn, falling northwest of Kemmel Ridge. The *Staffelführer* of *Jasta* 36, Ltn d R Heinrich Bongartz, was severely wounded in the same fight, losing his left eye. His place at the head of *Jasta* 36 was taken by Richard Plange from *Jasta* B, who was made permanent commander on 16 May. However, he would be killed only three days later.

By the beginning of May the famous *Jasta* 'Boelcke' was down to just five pilots due to transfers and losses incurred in the heavy fighting of April. Fortunately, the Kemmel Offensive had ceased on the 1st, allowing *Jasta* B some breathing space as it began to re-equip with the first of the superb new Fokker D VIIs. Nonetheless, on 3 May Carl Bolle was again successful, shooting down a Sopwith from No 73 Sqn south of Bailleul. The RAF unit lost two Camel pilots around midday, one killed and another made a PoW. At 1410 hrs, *Jasta* 'Boelcke' tackled a group of DH 9s from No 98 Sqn on a bombing raid on Menin. Once again Bolle's fire was accurate, for as he pummelled DH 9 C6101, it started to break apart then fell in flames. Lts R A Holiday and C B Whyte both perished.

Bolle was certainly on a 'hot streak'. On the morning of the 8th elements of JG III encountered SEs from No 1 Sqn, and Bolle wounded Lt J C Wood in SE 5a C6408 – the RAF airman was taken prisoner south of St Eloi. At 1420 hrs that same day, the triplanes of *Jasta* 'Boelcke' scrapped with Camels of No 43 Sqn, and Bolle and Fritz Kempf both tallied victories – the tenth for the *Staffelführer*. It was the fourth for Kempf, who was flying Dr I 493/17.

The *Jasta* commander made it 11 confirmed on 19 May 1918. No 206 Sqn's de Havillands were making a bombing raid when the *Staffel*

Fritz Kempf used Dr I 493/17 to claim his fourth victory on 8 May 1918, and this photograph likely shows that aeroplane. The upper wing was emblazoned with a black-bordered version of his name, and the middle wing bore a legend like that on his former Dr I. Note the black outline on the rudder (*A Imrie*)

Ltn Bolle prepares for flight in his Dr I 413/17 at Halluin-Ost in May 1918. The ratio of the crossbars on the fuselage and rudder was altered by this time to improve identification in the air, but the wing crosses retained their old style. The central fuselage band was in the yellow colour of Bolle's *Kürassier-Regiment von Seydlitz* Nr 7, bordered by the black and white Prussian colours. Bolle preferred a broad lap-strap to the usual shoulder-strap harness, and had an Oigee telescopic sight fitted to his Dr I. Note the early Fokker D VII in the background. Bolle chalked up his seventh and eighth victories on 3 May, followed by two more five days later (*A Imrie*)

intercepted them at 0820 hrs. Bolle destroyed DH 9 C6159 southwest of Zonnebeke, although he called it a 'Bristol' in his combat report. This day No 206 Sqn lost four de Havillands in two separate raids. Bolle and the rest of the *Jasta* would soon come to know and recognise the DH 9, which he reported was much faster then his Fokker triplane. He described one combat over the Ypres Salient when nine DH 9s were attacked by seven triplanes from *Jasta* B;

'I had targeted the leader's aircraft, flying ahead and in the middle, but I, however, left my course during my *Staffel*'s attack toward the front.

'The opponent, flying cleverly, let me go ahead and plunge into the wedge of his formation, and he had me completely surrounded before my comrades could get there. The concentrated fire from 18 machine guns totally covered my machine so that I had to bid farewell downwards – after I could only get off a brief burst at the enemy lead aircraft – with a shot up fuel tank and a badly shredded aeroplane. I believe, though, that I had noticed that this enemy aircraft – at the moment in which I let myself spin – had begun to smoke. At the same time the *Staffel*'s dogfight against the English squadron began.'

Bolle wrote that he counted 42 hits on his triplane. All of the *Jasta* pilots returned and glumly reported that the de Havillands had escaped, but several must have been badly shot up. No confirmed victories were achieved. Nonetheless, Bolle happily recounted that a few days later a captured DH 9 crew reported that their squadron had been badly mistreated by a triplane squadron. They described *Jasta* B's markings exactly, according to Bolle, and had lost five machines in crash landings, with a number of casualties.

Fortunately, some replacements for the depleted *Jasta* arrived throughout the month of May, including 20-year-old Ltn d R Ernst Bormann, who reported in from a brief stay at *Jasta* 12 on the 4th. He would prove a formidable addition to the unit. Ltn d Rs Johann Heemsoth and Wilhelm Suer were also posted in during the month.

On 9 May the highly experienced Ltn Alfred Lindenberger arrived from *Jastaschule* II. Born in Stuttgart on 22 April 1897, he had already won the Württemberg Silver Military Merit Medal as an infantryman in 1915. Flying as an observer with Fl Abt (A) 234 in 1917, he had claimed three French SPADs shot down. Two of these claims had been made with Vzfw Kurt Jentsch as his pilot – an airman who would later fly with *Jasta*

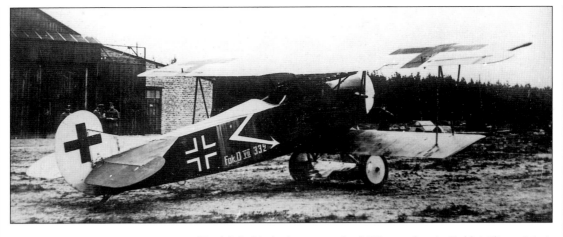

In late May *Jasta* 'Boelcke' began re-equipping with new Fokker D VIIs, and by mid-June most of the triplanes were gone. D VII 332/18 was finished in the Fokker 'streaky' finish on the fuselage and had five-colour printed fabric on the wings. *Staffel* markings consisted of the black/white tail and the white nose section, and the pilot's emblem was the lightning bolt on the fuselage. Circumstantial evidence suggests that this aircraft may have been flown by Otto Löffler

Bäumer's mechanics work on his Dr I 204/17. In its final guise, this triplane displayed *Balkenkreuze* and had the outer ends of all three wings painted black, with red and white trim. The cabane struts were also decorated in black and white, and some of the black paint has worn off the cowling

'Boelcke'. Lindenberger received Württemberg's Gold Military Merit Medal for his work as an observer on 4 January 1918.

On 18 May Ltn d R Hermann Frommherz returned to *Jasta* B following his spell instructing in the Lübeck flying school. He was no doubt happy to be back in action, and was perhaps spurred on to new effort. He would really begin to perform soon.

Between 21 and 24 May JG III continued its nomadic ways as it moved south to Vivaise aerodrome in the 7. *Armee* for the next offensive. The airfield was located ten kilometres northwest of Lâon, opposite French positions. *Jasta* 'Boelcke' had already left some of its Dr Is at AFP 4 as more D VIIs were taken on strength. The German offensive on the Aisne was scheduled to start on 27 May, and for the first time in its history *Jasta* 'Boelcke' would be opposed mostly by French airmen in the coming weeks.

Two days into the offensive, on 29 May, Carl Bolle chalked up his 12th victory with a French SPAD shot down at Soissons. His opponent was apparently an American from the Lafayette Flying Corps, Cpl Clarence Shoninger of *Escadrille* SPA99 (see *Osprey Aviation Elite Units 17 - SPA 124 Lafayette Escadrille* for further details). He had been attempting to drive off German reconnaissance aeroplanes when he was jumped by *Jasta* 'Boelcke' and came down wounded near a German flak battery. He was quickly taken prisoner.

However, that same day the *Staffel* lost one of its most valuable pilots. At this time Paul Bäumer had somehow acquired a rare Pfalz D VIII for his own use (see *Osprey Aircraft of the Aces 71 - Pfalz Aces of World War 1* for further details). This *Rara avis* was equipped with a 160 hp Siemens-Halske counter-rotary engine. Pehaps his preference for the manoeuvrability of rotary-engined fighters had something to do his choice, as the rest of his unit was re-equipping with in-line engined Fokker D VIIs. His Pfalz was suitably decorated with all the

At some point *circa* late May 1918, Paul Bäumer acquired a Pfalz D VIII fighter powered by the 160 hp Siemens-Halske Sh III counter-rotary engine – very possibly this was 124/18. This was almost certainly the only D VIII at *Jasta* 'Boelcke', and is perhaps indicative of Bäumer's status and his preference for light rotary-engined aircraft. Bäumer is seen at left with his Pfalz D VIII, which was marked with the usual *Staffel* colours of black and white on the cowling and tail. The oil that has liberally spewed out through the cooling holes in the cowling may indicate some engine trouble

usual *Staffel* and personal insignia, but he probably did not get to fly it for very long.

Bäumer had apparently gone out on a late afternoon/evening flight, *probably* in his Pfalz D VIII. Perhaps he was trying to acquaint himself with the new front. At about 2230 hrs he was returning to the still-unfamiliar airfield at Vivaise. It seems that in the darkness of the late hour he misjudged his landing and crashed. Bäumer was alive, but had sustained a complicated lower jaw fracture. He was initially taken to *Feld-Lazarett* (field hospital) Nr 602, and on 12 June was moved to the Aaper Wald Clinic in Düsseldorf, which apparently specialised in maxillofacial wounds. There, one of his fellow patients was Lothar von Richthofen, who had suffered his own severe jaw injuries when his Dr I crashed on 13 March 1918. Bäumer would not return to action until mid-September.

On 30 May both Alfred Lindenberger and Ernst Bormann put in claims for French Breguet 14 B2 bombers. Lindenberger's Breguet was later confirmed as shot down at Villers-Cotterets. However, Bormann had to

Bäumer's Pfalz D VIII was identified by a red-white-black chevron marking similar to the personal insignia on his Fokker Dr I. This personal emblem necessitated the overpainting of the national cross insignia, which was repainted further aft. On 29 May 1918, Bäumer crashed badly on the new *Staffel* airfield at Vivaise, suffering jaw injuries that put him out of action for several months. He may have been flying this D VIII at the time

be satisfied with a *zur Landung gezwungen*, since his victim landed just behind French lines at Teille, near Laon. There was a bit of a question about confirmation for Lindenberger's victory as well, for his victim of this day (30 May) was eventually confirmed as his fifth victory, while his next victim (on 1 June) was confirmed as his fourth! Although the Breguet 14 was a tough opponent, capable of absorbing a good deal of punishment, six of the two-seaters were lost on 30 May.

As noted on 1 June, Lindenberger downed another Breguet 14 B2 at Priez, and another Breguet was confirmed as falling to Ltn d R Heemsoth on the 2nd. Concerning the unit's activities on this new sector, Carl Bolle displayed the typical German anti-French prejudice when he wrote;

'At the end of May, *Jagdgeschwader* III – and with it the "Boelcke" *Staffel* – was transferred to the area around Laon. Now the *Staffel* had to finally show what it had learned in the meantime. For the time being, they had exclusively Frenchmen as opponents, who, with their well-known restraint in the air, made them difficult to catch. As a result of our rapid advances at Soissons and Fismes, where they had lost their airfields during the first days of the offensive on the Marne, the enemy's aerial activities were utterly meaningless. Only slowly did they adjust to the new, stronger German air force. Greater awareness was now necessary, and it took many unsuccessful patrols to even meet an opponent in the air, or to force a dogfight, not to mention achieving a victory.

'With the new French aerial forces being moved up, and especially with the appearance of Englishmen and Americans, the *Staffel*, however, got an opponent worthy of a fight. It had, in the meantime, become a unified whole once again, and was the equal of any opponent.'

Bolle was no doubt referring to the coming of the formidable *Division Aérienne (Escadre de Combat* Nos 1 and 2) in the middle of June, along with some experienced RAF units. At the beginning of July the American 1st Pursuit Group also arrived in the area.

Hermann Frommherz finally achieved his third confirmed victory on 3 June when he downed a SPAD at Ancienville. This was his first success since April 1917, and now that he 'had his eye in', there would be no stopping him. Another confirmed SPAD was recorded by Bolle on the same day, at Faubourg. The *Staffelführer* brought his total to 14 with a Breguet at Fresnes on the 4th.

Hermann Frommherz returned to *Jasta* 'Boelcke' on 18 May 1918, and is pictured here in a triplane which has had additional sights fitted. He soon resumed his scoring in rapid fashion, picking up his third victory on 3 June and his fourth six days later

These colourful *Jasta* 'Boelcke' triplanes photographed in May 1918 display a variety of personal insignia. At right, the Dr I with the black(?) and white 'diamond' fuselage band and sawtooth strut décor is thought to have been flown by Hermann Frommherz. Third from right is probably Dr I 157/17, which bore striped decoration on both its fuselage and interplane struts. To the left of it is Vallendor's 195/17, with his white *V* emblems. Note the two different patterns of black/white tail identification

JG III moved yet again on 6 June, and *Jasta* 'Boelcke' transferred to Mont Soissons Ferme, still with the 7. *Armee*. Three days later both Bolle and Frommherz shot down SPADs, and Frommherz had doubled his victory score in less than a week. On the 14th Bolle brought down another Breguet 14 B2 over Laversine. This may well have been a bomber from *Escadrille* BR29, flown by American Cpl Robert L Moore and Lt Guy Giguel. The French bombardier was reportedly killed.

On 16 June the *Jagdstaffel* seems to have flown rather far afield from their normal hunting grounds and gone poaching in the territory of *Jagdgeschwader* Nr II. Their claims are recorded at Bus-la-Mésière and south of Roye. Apparently the *Jasta* attacked DH 4s and DH 9s from No 27 Sqn, but the RAF bombers also came under fire from *Jagdstaffeln* 5 and 15. Bolle, Heemsoth and Ltn d R Wilhelm Suer of *Jasta* B all claimed de Havillands and received credit. No 27 Sqn was badly treated, losing three aircraft – one of them in flames – while another managed to reach home with a dead observer and wounded pilot. *Jasta* 15 of JG II put in its own competing claims and got five victories from the day.

In the middle of June *Jagdstaffel* 'Boelcke' took on the role of a *Schlachtstaffel*, participating in low-level assaults against troops to help stem the enemy tide. Bolle wrote, 'On 18 June, American infantry, attacked by the *Staffel*, was halted and dashed apart, along with the shooting down of a ground attack aircraft (unconfirmed)'.

In the month of June the *Jasta* attained a very respectable 13 victories. Carl Bolle complained, 'There would have been even more, but the *Staffel* was only able to take-off one to two times a day due to the lack of fuel created by difficulties in supply'. During these days and weeks, comments of this kind are to be found in the war diary, this being a common lament of many *Jagdstaffeln* in the summer of 1918.

JULY 1918

Ltn Gerhard Bassenge returned to *Jasta* B in July, having recovered from the wounds he sustained on 6 November 1917. Another new pilot to arrive during the month was Carl Bolle's brother Hermann, who displayed a distinct family resemblance.

The newcomer Ernst Bormann displayed promise with his first victory on 3 July, when he shot down a SPAD at Noroy, behind the German lines. His opponent is believed to have been Lt *Comte* Sanche de Gramont de Coigny, the commander of *Escadrille* N471 of the Paris Defence Group.

On 5 July *Jasta* 'Boelcke' had its first encounter with American opponents, and things did not go well for the 'Yanks' just one day after their national holiday. A patrol of six Nieuport 28s from the new 95th Aero Squadron of the 1st Pursuit Group, led by Capt John Mitchell, left

their field in the morning. Two of the Nieuports dropped out of the patrol, which soon ran into five or six D VIIs from *Jasta* 'Boelcke' and had what 1Lt Waldo Heinrichs called their 'first big fight' in his diary. Capt Harold R Buckley, later an ace with the 95th, wrote in his history of the squadron;

'We began our active work again and discovered that we had landed in a hornets' nest of Fokkers with death-dealing stings of lead. First to test the mettle of our new opponents were Mitchell, Heinrichs, Rhodes and Thompson, who hopped off early in the morning. Poor Thompson was making his first patrol, and didn't have a chance. He went down in flames with the first burst of the enemy guns. The other three put up a terrible fight against odds of two-to-one. Rhodes went down. By breakfast time they (Mitchell and Heinrichs) were back at the airdrome with their ships looking like sieves and a lurid tale for the rest of us.'

1Lt Carlyle 'Dusty' Rhodes was lucky to survive as a PoW, but 1Lt Sidney P Thompson died in his flaming Nieuport. Bolle and Frommherz received credit for the Nieuports, making Frommherz an ace.

On 15 July the final German offensive of the war was launched against the French around Rheims, on the Marne River. The German name for this was Operation *Friedensturm* (the 'Peace Offensive'), while the French called it the Second Battle of the Marne. After a four-hour bombardment, the Germans attacked on both sides of Rheims. The eastern attack broke against the French Army, but between Rheims and Château Thierry the German ground forces made significant progress. *Jasta* 'Boelcke' was in the thick of it, with Frommherz downing another Nieuport 28 that crashed in Allied lines. In the afternoon JG III was also in combat with

This photograph of the well-tonsured men of *Jasta* 'Boelcke' was probably taken sometime in early July 1918. They are, from left to right, Johann Heemsoth, Hermann Frommherz, Ernst Bormann, Eberhard von Gudenberg (OzbV), *Staffelführer* Karl Bolle, Fritz Kempf, Mynereck, Hermann Bolle (displaying quite a family resemblance to brother Karl) and Alfred Lindenberger

Camels from No 54 Sqn, with Bolle successfully claiming a Camel down at Dormans at 1400 hrs.

The heavy fighting continued on the 16th, with Bolle, Bormann and Frommherz all credited with 'Bristols'. With the confused fighting going on over a battle area – to say nothing of the poor aircraft identification endemic to pilots on *both* sides – these victories are impossible to correlate with RAF losses. Most likely these were in fact DH 9s, as several de Havilland bomber units did see some combat and casualties.

By 18 July the Second Battle of the Marne was over, and the Allies counter-attacked in what became known as the Battle of Château Thierry (or the Aisne-Marne Operation). That day Bolle was back in action, shooting up a Breguet at Ferté Henelles Ferme, and then a SPAD XIII at Beuvardes. The SPAD pilot has been identified as Lt Pierre Daire from *Escadrille* SPA159, who went missing this day. The French air forces suffered very heavy casualties during the offensive and counter-attack, and several Breguets were lost on 18 July. However, one Breguet crew managed to wound *Staffelführer* Bolle's brother Hermann on this same day, and he left for the hospital. It is believed he later returned to the unit.

Also on the 18th, *Jasta* 'Boelcke' transferred to Vauxcère, northwest of Fismes. It would soon be followed by the rest of JG III. Although the *Jasta* pilots were starting to feel overwhelmed by the masses of Allied aircraft they encountered, victories could still be obtained. During the evening of 22 July, the *Staffel* bounced a group of 'Sopwiths' – probably Camels from No 73 Sqn. Bolle shot down one of them near Coincy for his 25th confirmed victory. He was certainly in *Pour le Mérite* territory now.

Furthermore, his *Staffel* was clearly doing its job superbly. Late in the day on 25 July, a flight of six Sopwith Camels from No 43 Sqn was led over Fère-en-Tardenois by Capt C F King MC DFC. They saw a group of RAF bombers, with Camel escorts from No 73 Sqn, entangled in a swirling dogfight with some Fokker D VIIs. Capt King led his patrol down onto the hostile aircraft, and in the confused fighting he reported seeing one machine go down in flames and two more break asunder in the air. Sadly for King, these were all Camels from his flight.

Bolle and Frommherz were surely in their best form these days, for they each sent down one of the Camels, as did Gerhard Bassenge for his

Fokker D VIIs of *Jasta* 'Boelcke' show off their Prussian tail décor in the summer of 1918. Comparison with the photograph of 332/18 (seen on page 98) again reveals two opposite patterns of black/white markings on the tails, which probably served as *Kette* identification. From left to right are Ltn d R Johann Heemsoth, Ltn Karl Bolle, unknown, Gefr Mynereck and unknown (*A Imrie*)

number three. No 43 Sqn's Lt R E Meredith was killed, and Lts F S Coghill and N Wilson were both made PoWs, although the latter would die from his wounds on 18 October.

Three days after this memorable day, Bolle and Frommherz again scored. This time two Salmson 2A2 reconnaissance two-seaters from the rookie American 12th Aero Squadron suffered the attention of *Jasta* 'Boelcke's' formidable twosome. One crew was killed after falling near Villers-sur-Fère, while the other also came down at Sergy with a dead observer. One of these was considered the 250th victory of *Jasta* 'Boelcke' – the unit was moving up fast.

Success has its price, and in this case Hermann Frommherz' meteoric rise in the victory standings resulted in his departure from *Jasta* 'Boelcke' – similar to von Richthofen, von Tutschek and others. Surely Bolle would miss the formidable airman, but Frommherz was merely being transferred to *Jasta* 27 within JG III as acting commander. He would be named as permanent leader in August, and continue to add to his tally through to the end of the war. Frommherz survived with 32 victories, although he missed out on a well-deserved 'Blue Max' due to the armistice.

On 30 July the *Geschwader* resumed its peripatetic existence and moved to Chambry, north of Laon. The very next day the *Jasta* commander despatched a SPAD XIII for his 28th confirmed claim. Bolle had every reason to be happy with his own performance, and that of his *Staffel*, which had accounted for 18 opponents in July to bring its tally to 252. However, the tide of the ground war had turned. The *Geschwader,* not to mention the rest of Germany's forces, would soon be on the defensive.

Sometime in July 1918, Gerhard Bassenge returned to the *Staffel* – this photograph was taken between that time and the departure of Hermann Frommherz for command of *Jasta* 27 on July 29. These men are, from left to right, Alfred Frey, Alfred Lindenberger, Otto Löffler, Wilhelm Suer (with cigar), Mynereck (in rear), Bassenge, Eberhard von Gudenberg (OzbV), Ernst Bormann, Karl Bolle, Frommherz and Johann Heemsoth

SUCCESS IN RETREAT

By the start of August *Jasta* 'Boelcke' had a magnificent record and a proud *esprit de corps*. The unit's heritage and distinguished lineage were still celebrated. At this time Alfred Lindenberger made contact with his old pilot from his days in Fl Abt (A) 234, Vzfw Kurt Jentsch, who was now flying with *Jasta* 61. Lindenberger invited him over to Chambry for a visit at the end of July. Jentsch described his brief time with the unit in his book *Jagdflieger im Feuer*;

'I flew to Chambry. Immediately after landing I was introduced to the pilots of *Jagdstaffel* "Boelcke", to which Lindenberger belongs.

'*Jasta* "Boelcke" is led by Ltn Bolle and belongs to JG III, whose commander is Oblt Loerzer, a Knight of the *Pour le Mérite*. Under his energetic leadership, the *Geschwader* has developed splendidly.

'Ltn Lindenberger took me to the mess for coffee. The rectangular rooms made an impression of picture perfect cleanliness. Tablecloths as white as blossoms, uniform coffee service and flowers in vases, cleverly spread about, gave the tables a friendly look. *Staffelführer* Bolle sits at the head of the table.

'Next to his place sits the telephone, which is indispensable to a successful air service. On the walls hang pictures of the fallen. First was Hptm Boelcke and Oblt Kirmaier, then came Ltn Voss, Ltn Max *Ritter* von Müller, Ltn Walter von Bülow and many others.

'At one time our most important combat pilots began their careers in this *Jagdstaffel* – they absorbed Hptm Boelcke's teachings which brought about their unforeseen blossoming. Rittmeister Manfred *Freiherr* von Richthofen greatly exceeded his teacher and master through his exemplary number of victories. I have to think of all these things because they immediately come to mind when one is a guest here. Lindenberger informed me, as we bade farewell, that Ltn Bolle would apply for my transfer to *Jagdstaffel* "Boelcke". I was very happy about this.'

Jentsch would eventually succeed in joining *Jasta* B. Like most airmen, he began the war on the ground as an infantryman. After successfully managing a switch to the air service, he attended the *Fliegerschule* at Niederneuendorf, then went on to FEA 1 in 1916. He was eventually ordered to AFP 13 as a single-seater pilot. Jentsch was attached to the *Kampfstaffel des* AFP 13 and soon travelled to Hudova to provide air support for the Bulgarian Army, and he apparently gained three confirmed and five unconfirmed victories. He returned to France in 1917 and flew with *Jasta* 1, downing a SPAD on 23 June. In August 1917 he switched to Rumpler two-seaters in Fl Abt (A) 234, then in January Jentsch transferred to *Jasta* 61.

At some point in August Oblt Kurt von Griesheim also joined *Jasta* B.

The first week of August was comparatively quiet. The Allies were secretly preparing for a decisive offensive on the Amiens front. The attack by the British 4th Army and the French 1st Army would take place along a stretch of the Front from Morlancourt to La Neuville. At 0420 hrs on 8 August, the storm broke as 2000 guns opened up. Aided by a heavy fog, the troops advanced, assisted by large numbers of tanks. They made

On 13 August 1918, Vzfw Kurt Jenstch arrived at *Jagdstaffel* 'Boelcke' from *Jasta* 61. He had flown as Alfred Lindenberger's pilot when they both served in Fl Abt (A) 234, where this photograph was taken (note the arm patch). Lindenberger managed to get his old friend posted to *Jasta* B, and Jentsch brought a wealth of flying experience to his new post

unprecedented gains, partially because the RAF carried out a great deal of valuable cooperation with the troops and tanks on the ground. JG III claimed victories on the 8th but *Jasta* 'Boelcke' was scoreless.

The intense aerial action continued on 9 August. Bolle shot down an RE 8 from No 6 Sqn near Rosières in the afternoon. That same day the unit became directly involved in the ground fighting. Bolle reported;

'English infantry, along with Americans, attacked the village of Rosières with ground attack aeroplanes and tanks. The tanks, covered by a range of hills, led against the village, but were not observed by German artillery and thus were not fired upon. After the ground attack aircraft retreated before our German *Staffel,* we dived as a unit onto the tanks and attacked them with machine guns. After the third attack, the artillery (which had in the meantime become aware of the tanks because of the continuous dives of our aircraft) laid down destructive fire in the area concerned. After a short time three tanks were burning, two others remained motionless and the rest had retreated.'

In the evening of the 9th, Löffler shot down an FK 8 from No 35 Sqn for his third confirmed claim.

Two days later Bolle claimed a 'SPAD two-seater' that was actually a Salmson 2A2 for his number 30. Germans frequently had trouble identifying the differences between the SPAD XI, Breguet 14 and

This photograph of Karl Bolle with his Fokker D VII was taken in July 1918 following his first mention in the Army Communiqué. The D VII displayed his usual black, white and yellow bands and two white stripes on the top wing. The *Feldschnalle* (ribbons bar) on Bolle's chest includes the ribbons of the Iron Cross 2nd Class, the Württemberg Friedrich Order 2nd Class and Military Merit Cross 2nd Class from Mecklenburg-Schwerin. Bolle would soon add the 'Hohenzollern' and, on 28 August, the *Pour le Mérite*

Salmson 2A2. The *Staffel* pounced on several Salmsons from the American 88th Aero Squadron flying a photo-reconnaissance patrol. The crew of 1Lt J H McClendon and 2Lt C Plummer were both killed, and two other crews were badly shot up.

On 13 August Jentsch was posted to the *Staffel*. He arrived at Chambry and reported to Bolle;

'Afterwards, I have to introduce myself to the *Geschwaderführer*. The office is located very near. I report to Oblt Dahlmann, the *Geschwader* adjutant, who has just come in, and he leads me to the *Geschwaderführer*. Oblt Loerzer, the commander of JG III, is sitting in a high-backed armchair at his desk. As I click my heels, he glances up. I report, according to regulations. "Pilot Vzfw Jentsch, from *Jagdstaffel* 61, transferred to *Jagdgeschwader* III".

'Oblt Loerzer acknowledges and welcomes me. The sun floods the room, its rays mirroring themselves in the *Pour le Mérite* he is wearing. The charming and friendly manner with which I am received has immediately won me over to the commander. I have never before been greeted so affably and in such a relaxed manner by an officer in a superior position. After several questions concerning my training and previous positions of command held, I am dismissed.

'After lunch, it's off to the front. Ltn Lindenberger is flying next to me. We fly over our old hunting grounds around Soissons, in which we are still "at home" even today. Both far and wide, there is nothing to be seen of the Frenchmen. Only the enemy flak does not fail to appear. Clouds of shrapnel, white like cotton balls, burst forth around us and fade.

'I have already gotten acquainted with my "new" Fokker D VII – it is, though, no longer really new, but is in good shape. For the top (paint) coat they've chosen sky blue – only the horizontal stabilizer surfaces and the fuselage end are painted in black and white, half and half. This is the same for the elevators. Black and white are the recognition colours of *Jasta* "Boelcke".

During the Battle of Amiens, JG I – the 'Richthofen' *Geschwader* – had suffered such heavy losses that the unit's war diary for 13 August read, 'Due to the heavy losses of the last few days, the *Geschwader* was condensed to one *Staffel*. Close cooperation with *Jagdgeschwader* III and *Jagdgruppe* "Greim"'. This photograph from Ernst Udet's book *Mein Fliegerleben* reflects that situation, as JG I adjutant (and former *Jasta* B OzbV) Karl Bodenschatz at left and Udet (centre) confer with *Jasta* 'Boelcke' CO Karl Bolle at right. Between Udet and Bolle is a heavily retouched view of Bolle's D VII, and beyond Bodenschatz at left is another D VII from *Jasta* B bearing a black zigzag lightning bolt emblem

'In the evening hours, the *Staffel* is sent out again. In exemplary order, to the right and the left of the lead aircraft, formed up towards the back, we move over the Front. The crosses on the wings stand out very clearly on each machine. The white edges of the national markings glow in the rays of the setting sun. Below us, the ground fighting rages – drumfire is being laid on the German lines. The aerial space over the Front, however, belongs to us. Safe and sound, we land back at Chambry airfield after a flight of almost two hours.'

On 18 August Lindenberger claimed a Breguet, and Bormann sent an AR 1 two-seater from *Escadrille* AR268 down at Nouvron. Pilot Sous Lt Pierre Paquier was killed while his observer Lt Marcel Tournaire was wounded. That same day 'Fritz' Kempf bade farewell to *Jasta* 'Boelcke'. He had notched up four victories, flown with the *Jasta* for 15 months and did a commendable job as a *Kette* leader. He was sent off to *Jastaschule* I as an instructor, and survived the war.

On the 20th Lindenberger claimed another of the unfortunate ARs west of Champs for his seventh kill. On the 21st Löffler bagged a Breguet in the same location for his fourth victory. The Breguet may have been a machine from Br131. The crew of pilot Adj Dejean de St Marcel and observer MdL Jean-Baptiste Gurby were both wounded, but managed to make it home. On the 22nd Bormann downed a SPAD XIII for his own fourth victory.

EMERCHICOURT

Once again the *Geschwader* was planning a move, this time back to the British front in the 17. *Armee*. The *Staffel* would now be based at Emerchicourt, south of Aniche. On the 25th Jentsch prepared to fly off with the others:

'The new day breaks. It is raining, and thick mist lies over the earth. With the others, *Jagdstaffel* "Boelcke" waits for the orders to take-off. Oblt

An unidentified *Jasta* 'Boelcke' pilot poses with his D VII and groundcrew. The Fokker shows off the white nose that was part of the *Staffel* livery. In the hands of experienced pilots like Bäumer, Bolle, Bormann, Lindenberger and Löffler, the BMW-engined Fokker D VII proved a potent weapon in late 1918

Loerzer, the *Geschwader* commander, gives the order to take-off and roars away first, and then it is our turn, under the leadership of Ltn Bolle. One machine after another joins the formation. In this misty air it is difficult to keep in contact. Like a shadow, Ltn Lindenberger's Fokker lifts up, flying to the right of me. At tree level, the *Geschwader* races ahead, flying over the streets and villages. Of the other aircraft, one only occasionally sees their wheels when they drop downward out of the fog – propeller backwash from those flying in front of us causes turbulence, forcing us to wrestle with our control sticks.

'It becomes light over St Quentin. Soon after the foggy region is behind us – sunshine surges around our aeroplanes. The *Geschwader* flies superbly together, so no *Staffel* lags behind. Even fog and rain were not able to loosen the discipline of the *Geschwader*. Always, we head north.

'Our airfield is called Emerchicourt, and is located between Arras and Lens, ten kilometres to the southeast of Douai. The *Geschwader* reaches Emerchicourt, and one *Staffel* after another lands. The airfield is broad and well situated – one can take-off and land from all quarters of the sky. In the southern part of Aniche – a small town, and the intersection of several railway lines – we take up our pilots' quarters.'

25-year-old Ltn Fritz Hoffmann was posted to the *Staffel* on the 25th. Despite his unusually small size, he had served in the infantry, but now came back to the front as a pilot. Jentsch wrote;

'The chief mechanic has grief with him because he cannot reach the controls. When one is hardly 150 cm tall, such things are somewhat difficult. With the aid of a welded steel pipe frame, the controls are lengthened for the small leutnant. After dinner, Hoffmann sits down at the piano that stands in our mess' winter garden. It is a joy to hear him play – music diverts and relaxes.'

Ltn Alfred Lindenberger smiles from the cockpit of his striped D VII (OAW) 4453/18. Lindenberger was another prolific scorer in late 1918, achieving two victories in August, two more in September and two more by 1 November to bring his total to 12. His Fokker was one of those interned at Nivelles, and shows up in several photographs

The pilot of this upended D VII of the 'Boelcke' *Staffel* is unfortunately unidentified. The personal emblem of a black(?) ace of spades appeared on a dark-bordered white band. The usual *Jasta* colours were applied to the tail surfaces

This photograph was taken to commemorate the award of the *Pour le Mérite* to Oblt Karl Bolle on 28 August 1918, when his score stood at 31. These men are, from left to right, Mynereck, Otto Löffler, Fritz Heinz, Fritz Hoffmann, Eberhard von Gudenberg (OzbV), Bolle, Kurt von Griesheim, Franz Klausenberg, Gerhard Bassenge, Kurt Jentsch and Alfred Lindenberger. Fritz Hoffmann was all of 150 cm tall, and special adjustments had to made to the controls in his Fokker D VII (*A Imrie*)

In the late afternoon of the 26th a patrol from the American 17th Aero Squadron ran into the *Geschwader* near Bourlon Wood, and disaster followed for the Camel outfit. The Americans lost no fewer than six aircraft to JG III. Bolle and *Jasta* B newcomer Fritz Heinz each claimed one out of the carnage. Frommherz, now leading *Jasta* 27, shot down three. Out of the six Americans shot down, three died and three were captured.

On 28 August Bolle received his *Pour le Mérite*, and there was great joy in the *Staffel*. An evening celebration was in order, and the staff of JG III and several other notables showed up. Jentsch wrote;

'Our mess looks very festive. The tables are decorated with flowers and arranged in a horseshoe shape. The tablecloth gleams white, the glasses and silverware have been polished, spick and span. Nearby, in the winter

garden, von Gudenberg has set up a small band from an infantry regiment that is to entertain us with string music.

'In the glow of the light bulbs, the officers' *Pour le Mérites* are aglitter. The atmosphere is good from the start. The food is served, wine sparkles in the glasses.'

All in all it was a very festive evening, complete with cigars, wine and the cook's 'Epicurean delight', which was actually potato soup. Food was scarce in blockaded Germany and in its armed forces, but for a few hours the war was put aside.

BLACK SEPTEMBER

September 1918 was the most successful month in the history of *Jasta* B, surpassing the 30 aircraft downed in October 1916. The 2nd of the month would be the best day in the career of JG III.

2 September would be remembered as the 'Black Day' by American Camel pilots of the 148th Aero Squadron. *Jasta* B was responsible for the massacre – by the end of the action Bormann had three more Camels to his credit, Löffler two and Heinz one. 'A' and 'B' Flights of the 148th had flown across the lines to protect two-seaters when they were ambushed. It appears that Bormann shot down three aircraft from 'B' Flight, led by Capt Elliott W Springs, who was the only one who returned. Lt Field Kindley led 'A' Flight into the scrap to try to help, but both Kindley and Lt Jesse Creech were badly shot up by Löffler and barely made it back across the lines. Two Camel pilots were killed and two captured. Creech gave this account;

'I undertook to dive out of the swirling aeroplanes and climb to the top, but two Germans spied this manoeuvre and drove me back to the middle of the fight. Shortly after this I fell in on the tail of a Fokker, and just as I got my sights adjusted and let go a burst, all the instruments in front of my

The identity of this *Jasta* 'Boelcke' D VII remains unconfirmed. On the back of the original print in the Papenmeyer album, an unknown hand had written, 'My aircraft with which I shot down ten Englishmen'. The late historian A E Ferko was of the opinion that this D VII belonged to Otto Löffler. The black zigzag or lightning bolt insignia invites comparison with D VII 332/18 pictured previously (*Papenmeyer album*)

face began to disappear. I quickly kicked my right-hand rudder in, and when I turned my head, I found that two enemy fliers were sitting on my tail, pumping lead into my dashboard.

'The bullets, which had riddled my dashboard completely, wrecked my oil tank, and the engine of my Camel soon overheated and stopped. At 17,000 ft in the air, I had a problem on my hands to escape and glide into Allied territory. I was able to cross the Canal du Nord at a height of 100 ft, finally crashing into shell holes back of the line.'

Jentsch gave his own version of the action;

'It has been roaring away above us for the entire morning. English and American squadrons smash into our *Jagdstaffeln*. As long as we are in readiness, the fights will know no end. *Jasta* "Boelcke", too, records aerial victories. Ltn Bormann has shot down three Sopwith Camels, which broke apart. So that he would not feel alone, Ltn Löffler finishes off three (sic) others of the same type at Beugnatre. Ltn Heinz ends it with the shooting down of a "Tommy" at Boiry.'

The best evidence of their joy in fighting, and in the commitment from them all, is in the Army Despatch from 2 September 1918. In curt words, it makes the following announcement;

'We shot down 13 enemy balloons and 55 aircraft, 36 of which were over the Arras battlefield. Of these, JG III, under the leadership of Oblt Loerzer, brought down 26 aircraft.'

Paul Bäumer returned from his convalescence in early September and wasted no time in resuming his own chase for the 'Blue Max'. On 5 September he destroyed a Bristol, and would collect 15 more victories in that month alone. Here, Bäumer, at left, chats with a visiting relative identified as Kaspar Michaels in front of a Fokker D VII (*A Imrie*)

More successes lay ahead. On 3 September Lindenberger claimed a 'Bristol' at 1805 hrs near Combles, and a DH 9 from No 98 Sqn became Löffler's eighth kill. Bolle went on leave on 4 September, at about the same time he was promoted to oberleutnant. He left the unit under the acting command of Ltn d R Löffler. Paul Bäumer returned on the 4th, the same day Bormann shot down an SE at Pelves.

Unfortunately Jentsch was wounded on the 4th. He was flying highest in the *Jasta* formation when he saw a large formation of RAF fighters above and behind them. He recalled;

'A few seconds later, there was a rattling behind me. The first shots struck my Fokker and one of these hit my left side. Immediately banking, I saw the tracer threads spraying about me. In spite of this I did not leave my post.

'Blood was running down my left leg – I felt its warmth here and there. It was now 0835 hrs. The bullet wound was beginning to hurt, and because of this I had to fly back. Twenty minutes later our field at Emerchicourt came into view. I landed smoothly in spite of the fact that I could hardly move. I turned off the petrol and ignition. My mechanics lifted me out of my seat. My left leg had nearly gone stiff – it could hardly move, and the parachute upon which I had been sitting had been shredded by several hits. A hand's length to the right and my spine would have got it!'

Jentsch's war was over.

On the 5th Bäumer showed he was fully recovered by claiming a Bristol for his 23rd victory. The 6th was another day of multiple victories, with No 11 Sqn losing two 'Brisfits' to Löffler and Bäumer. A few hours later Bormann and Lindenberger fought it out with No 208 Sqn and both were credited with Camels as *Jasta* 'Boelcke's' total approached 280. There was a bit of a lull until the 14th, when an RE 8 was added to Bäumer's growing list. With 26 victories, he may well have been wondering where his own *Pour le Mérite* was.

Members of *Jagdstaffel* 'Boelcke', along with their canine friend, catch some late summer sun with a Fokker D VII backdrop. They are, from left to right, pilot Ltn d R Johann Heemsoth, OzbV Ltn von Gudenberg, Ltn d R Paul Bäumer and Bäumer's visiting relative Michaels (*A Imrie*)

On the 16th there was another flurry of confirmed claims, all 'Bristols'. Bäumer and the diminutive Fritz Hoffmann each got one, while Löffler got a double. Oblt Bolle returned from leave on the 18th, no doubt pleased to hear of his unit's successes, and to find it largely intact except for Jentsch.

On the 20th Bäumer started a spectacular streak of victories in this period of hectic combat. On that day he despatched a Camel, probably from No 203 Sqn. On the 21st he tallied three de Havillands, with one of these being a No 57 Sqn DH 4 that fell in flames near Bourlon Wood. Three days later, both Bäumer and Löffler were credited with DH types, with the former also adding another Camel to his score.

On 27 September the *Staffel* moved to Lieu St Amand airfield, still in the 17. *Armee*, but they would only tarry there three days. The *Jasta* B diary records an astounding *nine* victories on the 27th, giving the unit the best day in its history. Detailing each of the victories scored in September and October 1918 is beyond the scope of this book, and describing each one becomes repetitive and redundant – the terse accounts here cannot do justice to the sacrifice of brave men on both sides.

Perhaps it should be noted, however, that newcomer Uffz Karl Fervers destroyed a single-seater on the 27th, and Bormann also claimed two 'unknown types' that same day. Bassenge, Vallendor and Bäumer all contributed to the impressive tally. The 27th also saw the loss of Fritz Heinz to No 56 Sqn – the first fatal *Jasta* casualty since July, which in itself is a testament to the unit's level of efficiency.

The grisly statistics go on, with three more victims falling to the BMW-engined D VIIs of the 'Boelcke' *Staffel* on the 28th. Even neophytes were capable of benefiting from the qualities of the Fokker in September. On the 29th two relative tyros, Fervers and Vzfw Paul Keusen, both contributed to the total of five victories chalked up on the day. However it was still a deadly game, and the *Jasta* lost little Ltn Hoffmann, killed west of Cambrai. September's 'butcher's bill' totalled 46 victories, the highest monthly tally ever. On the last day of the month the unit retreated to Spultier airfield. Bolle wrote;

This *Jasta* 'Boelcke' pilot, seen with his D VII, remains unidentified. There is some suggestion he may have been Flgr Fritz Papenmeyer, the brother of Wilhelm, who was posted to the unit very late in the war. Aside from the usual *Staffel* markings, the aircraft bore a dark-bordered white band on the fuselage. This machine later turned up in RAF hands at Nivelles

Ltn d R Paul Bäumer was the top scorer of *Jasta* B, surpassing even Boelcke's total by achieving 43 confirmed victories by war's end. He was also the last *Staffel* member to receive the *Pour le Mérite,* the award being finally bestowed on 2 November 1918

'October was already being taken up by the commencement of withdrawal and frequent changes of base. Because of this, activities and successes were restricted. In the air, the opponent was now powerfully superior in numbers.'

The *Staffel* was well staffed with pilots by this time, including Fritz Papenmeyer, the brother of Wilhelm. Ltn d R Blunck and Ltn Schlack also joined the unit in October.

On 8 October the second Battle of Le Cateau began as the British 3rd and 4th Armies, as well as the 1st French Army, forced their way forward south of Cambrai. Bäumer and Fervers claimed Sopwiths that day, but no amount of German successes in the air could stem the Allied advance. The *Staffel* was forced to move to Lenz, by Mons, on the 10th as the 17. *Armee* retreated.

Bäumer's total had now reached 43. However, the ex-NCO pilot would never be given command of a *Jasta,* nor would he be awarded the 'Hohenzollern', which was usually the prerequisite for the *Pour le Mérite.* On 12 September he left the *Staffel* to attend the Fighter Trials at Adlershof. Bäumer was then posted to the Inspectorate of military aviation (*Idflieg*) and never returned to combat. His 'Blue Max' was awarded on 2 November 1918. Remaining in aviation postwar, he died when his aircraft crashed into the sea off Copenhagen on 15 July 1927.

The *Staffeln* were hampered by the lack of fuel, but they could still pose a threat. On 29 October new pilot Paul Blunck, together with Bormann, shot down two ground-strafing Camels from No 3 Sqn. The next day saw the heaviest aerial fighting of the entire war, and *Jasta* B downed six aeroplanes. They ambushed SEs from No 32 Sqn and knocked down three of them – aces Capt A Callender and Lt R Farquhar were both killed. Von Griesheim and Schlack both scored for the first time, along with several veteran pilots.

FINAL DAYS

On 4 November the last great aerial battles of the Great War were fought. Here, Bolle tells the story of that memorable day when the *Jasta* encountered the new and formidable Sopwith Snipes of No 4 Sqn AFC;

'And the finale. The Western Front was withdrawing towards the Antwerp-Meuse line. 4 November 1918 had arrived. In the morning the *Staffel* had been out on a short flight, and in the bitter cold at high altitude had polished off an English long-range reconnaissance aircraft and two fighters who were on the lookout for our own reconnaissance aeroplanes.

'At this time petrol was in very short supply, so we had to deploy our aircraft sparingly. It was 1430 hrs, and for five aircraft of the *Staffel*, there was enough fuel for 1½ hours of flight, which could be expended this day. The selection of the standby pilots had taken place.

'Then suddenly, shortly before 1500 hrs, there is flak artillery directed at a low altitude and rattling machine gun fire in a northwesterly direction. Soon, the well-trained eye catches sight of the English aerial forces that are invading our airspace and sweeping over roads used by columns on the march behind our lines.

'So the order is given to take off. The pilots climb into their machines and head at 100 and 200 metres height towards the spot where the enemy incursion had taken place. We only have these five aircraft, so it will not be easy. However, the enemy apparently has no great desire to close with the

The men of *Jasta* 'Boelcke' encountered the superb new Sopwith Snipe fighter during their final day of combat. The Snipe pilots were from No 4 Sqn AFC, and they suffered five casualties at the hands of the 'Boelcke' *Staffel*. This Snipe, E8184, is of the final production form, with balanced upper ailerons and a large fin and rudder

Just beyond the tail of an Albatros D Va, Lindenberger's OAW-built D VII 4453/18 heads a line-up of Fokkers at Nivelles, most of them from JG III. The third Fokker is 501/18 in the distinctive black/white stripes of *Jasta* 26, with another *Jasta* 'Boelcke' D VII fourth in line

Staffel rushing toward them in tight formation. They give up their operation and disappear as swiftly as possible behind their lines.

'The *Staffel* ascends between clusters of clouds in order to secure the sky above. Look there! Here comes the enemy's next wave of attack, roaring at exactly the right moment, just about to dive through the loose collection of clouds towards the earth with its roadways. But this time it will not be so easy. *Jasta* "Boelcke" has thrust itself between the enemy and the target.

'The *Staffel* makes a sharp turn. A German pilot fails to pay attention, is surprised and dives down in flames. The victorious Englishman himself follows 100 metres behind, having been shot down in flames by the *Staffel* commander. And then the actual battle commences.

'A far superior English fighter aeroplane, much better in climb and manoeuvrability than the Fokker D VIIs of *Jasta* "Boelcke", goes on the attack. The battle turns into a wild, mixed up melee. In any event, we have to stick it out, because if the *Staffel* yields here then the path will be clear for the English to attack our troops.

Fokker D VII (OAW) 4453/18 of Ltn Lindenberger is the central focus of this postwar photo at Nivelles. The striping on the fuselage just *might* have been yellow and black, inspired by the pilot's award of Württemberg's Gold Military Merit Medal. By the time this aeroplane was turned over to the RAF, its finish was distinctly degraded

Oblt Karl Bolle commanded *Jagdstaffel* 'Boelcke' through to war's end. The unit was officially credited with 336 victories during its distinguished career, 138 of them coming under Bolle's leadership. Some 31 of those were scored by Bolle himself (out of his total of 36), with the final four being attained on 4 November 1918

Some of the best available photographs of *Jasta* 'Boelcke' D VIIs were taken after the war at Nivelles, in Belgium, where many of the unit's Fokkers were reluctantly handed over to the British. RAF authorities have already begun to overpaint or remove the German national insignia from this D VII, which displayed a white *K* personal emblem along with a black-outlined arrow. Sadly, the *Jasta* 'Boelcke' pilot of this D VII remains unidentified

'The Englishmen remain above the Germans like rattling birds of prey. Again and again they dive down, shoot, zoom upwards and turn again, yet we cannot reach them with our inferior aircraft. However, through tricky flying we finally succeed in manoeuvering individual opponents down to our level and fasten upon them, wreaking destruction.

'The English squadron commander is finally hit and plummets down at the same time as one of his companions. This was the end of the fight. The battle had lasted a long time, and was one of the hardest that *Jasta* "Boelcke" had to endure in the final year of the war. The new type of aircraft would have given the enemy air service the superior edge throughout the Autumn and Winter months. In its first encounter *Jagdstaffel* "Boelcke" also managed to handle them.

'Our fuel supply for the day was used up and the *Staffel* returned home to its airfield. The result for this day was six aerial victories. It was the final day of combat for *Jasta* "Boelcke". Boelcke's teachings and his spirit were upheld till the bitter end.'

The Australians of No 4 Sqn lost five Snipes this day (four of them to Bolle), as two men were captured and three more killed. Two of the dead were T C R Baker and A Palliser, both aces. *Jasta* 'Boelcke' despatched six opponents in its final day of combat, in exchange for the death of Vzfw Keusen. The *Jasta* compiled a record of 336 victories for the entire war. This was balanced by 31 pilots killed in action, nine wounded, two captured and two killed in crashes. Their victory total was technically

CHAPTER SIX

118

Bolle's final BMW-engined Fokker D VII is seen at Nivelles after the armistice. When this aircraft was delivered to the Allies, it bore a young mechanic's inscription that stated 'With this machine 40 Englishmen were shot down'. An exaggeration, certainly, but perhaps a forgivable one

second to the 350 of *Jasta* 11, but *Jagdstaffel* 'Boelcke' was truly second to none in its prestige, proud lineage and its record of persevering through adversity.

The unit made its final retreat to Aniche on the 9th, and its fighting days were over. According to the conditions of the armistice of 11 November 1918, *Jagdgeschwader* III had to give up its D VIIs to the British at Nivelles. It was not easy to convince the angry pilots to comply with this order – some suggested that the aircraft be burned instead. Yet discipline was still maintained, and the pilots flew their cherished Fokkers to the collection centre with heavy hearts. The D VIIs arrived in perfect formation and taxied toward the British officials waiting for them. As the Fokkers slowly coasted to a stop, the Allied Commission officers could see that every D VII bore writing on the fuselage. As Bolle wrote;

'The handover followed. Each aircraft carried the glorious name of its pilot and the number of his victories. Thus they gave witness to the deeds which were accomplished with them.'

The serial number of this *Jasta* 'Boelcke' D VII in postwar British hands was 5109/18. The number was re-marked at the top of the rudder, and also chalked on the aft fuselage. The national insignia on the fuselage and rudder were crudely obscured with white paint. This BMW-engined D VII displayed personal band markings on the fuselage surprisingly similar to those on Lindenberger's machine, but less extensive

APPENDICES

APPENDIX 1

JAGDSTAFFEL 2/'BOELCKE' COMMANDERS

Commander	Dates of Command	Notes
Hptm Oswald Boelcke	27/8/16 to 22/9/16	illness
Oblt Günther Viehweger	22/9/16 to 23/9/16	stv
Hptm Oswald Boelcke	23/9/16 to 28/10/16	KIA, collision
Oblt Stefan Kirmaier	30/10/16 to 22/11/16	KIA
Oblt Karl Bodenschatz	22/11/16 to 29/11/16	stv
Hptm Franz Josef Walz	29/11/16 to 9/6/17	to *Jasta* 34b, CO
Ltn Fritz Otto Bernert	9/6/17 to 28/6/17	Leave
Ltn Otto Hunzinger	28/6/17 to 29/6/17	stv
Ltn Fritz Otto Bernert	29/6/17 to 8/7/17	Leave
Ltn Otto Hunzinger	8/7/17 to 9/7/17	stv
Ltn Fritz Otto Bernert	9/7/17 to 18/8/17	illness, to *Idflieg*
Ltn d R Erwin Böhme	18/8/17 to 9/9/17	Leave
Ltn d R Johannes Wintrath	9/9/17 to 18/9/17	stv
Ltn d R Erwin Böhme	18/9/17 to 24/10/17	Leave
Ltn d R Karl Gallwitz	24/10/17 to 30/10/17	stv
Ltn d R Erwin Böhme	30/10/17 to 29/11/17	KIA
Ltn Eberhard von Gudenberg	30/11/17 to 13/12/17	stv
Ltn Walter von Bülow-Bothkamp	13/12/17 to 6/1/18	KIA
Ltn Max Müller	6/1/18 to 9/1/18	stv, KIA
Ltn Theodor Cammann	10/1/18 to 26/1/18	stv
Ltn d R Otto Walter Höhne	26/1/18 to 20/2/18	to *Jastaschule* I
Ltn Carl (Karl) Bolle	20/2/18 to 4/9/18	Leave
Ltn d R Otto Löffler	4/9/18 to 18/9/18	stv
Oblt Carl Bolle	18/9/18 to 11/11/18	to end of war

Those who were temporary acting commanders are noted as stv (*stellvertreter*).

APPENDIX 2

ACES OF *JAGDSTAFFEL* 2 'BOELCKE'

Name	Victories in *Jasta* 'Boelcke'	Total Victories	Notes
Ltn d R Paul Bäumer	40	43	PLM
Oblt Carl Bolle	31	36	PLM
Ltn d R Werner Voss	28	48	PLM, KIA 23/9/17
Ltn d R Erwin Böhme	22	24	PLM, KIA 29/11/17
Hptm Oswald Boelcke	21	40	PLM, KIA 28/10/16
Oblt Fritz Otto Bernert	17	27	PLM, died 18/10/18
Ltn d R Ernst Bormann	16	16	
Rtm Manfred von Richthofen	16	80	PLM, KIA 21/4/18
Ltn d R Otto Löffler	15	15	
Ltn Max *Ritter* von Müller	11	36	PLM, KIA 9/1/18
Ltn d R Hermann Frommherz	10	29	
Ltn Alfred Lindenberger	8	11	
Ltn Gerhard Bassenge	7	7	
Ltn d R Richard Plange	7	7	KIA 19/5/18
Ltn d R Hermann Vallendor	6	6	
Ltn d R Erich König	6	6	KIA 2/4/17
Ltn d R Otto Höhne	6	6	
Ltn d R Hans Imelmann	6	6	KIA 23/1/17
Ltn Theodor Cammann	1	12	
Ltn Walter von Bülow-Bothkamp	0	28	PLM, KIA 6/1/18

PLM = *Pour le Mérite* recipient
KIA = killed in action

APPENDIX 3

NOTES ON SELECTED *JAGDSTAFFEL* 'BOELCKE' AIRCRAFT SERIAL NUMBERS

Aircraft	Pilot (if known)	Details
Fokker D III 352/16	Boelcke	Scored unit's first six victories in this aircraft
Albatros D I 384/16	Collin?	Prototype aircraft; possibly marked as *Co*
Albatros D I 390/16	Höhne	Marked *Hö*
Albatros D I 391/16	Büttner	Pilot PoW on 16/11/16 – marked as *Bü*
Albatros D I 426/16	Günther	Marked *G*, later *L* Reimann
Albatros D I 427/16	von Tutschek	Emergency landing 1/2/17
Albatros D I 438/16	von Tutschek	Test Flight 29/1/17
Albatros D II 386/16	Boelcke	Perhaps 14 victories; KIA 28/10/16
Albatros D II 491/16	Richthofen	Serial also recorded as 481/16
Albatros D II 1708/16	von Tutschek	Four test flights 26/1/17
SSW D I 3754/16		Delivered 12/4/17
Albatros D III 1925/16	Von Tutschek	Flown Jan/Feb 1917
Albatros D III 1982/16	Kinkel/Imelmann?	Imelmann KIA 23/1/17, according to war diary
Albatros D III 1994/16	Von Tutschek	1st victory 6/3/17
Albatros D III 2004/16	Von Tutschek	2nd victory 31/3/17
Albatros D III 2119/16	Bassenge	Marked black/white bands

Aircraft	Pilot (if known)	Details
Albatros D III 751/17	Hunzinger	Marked with *OH* on band
Albatros D III 790/17	Münz	KIA on 20/5/17
Albatros D III 795/17	Eggers	Crashed, unhurt
Albatros D III 796/17	Noth	PoW on 19/5/17 – green with yellow spots
Albatros D V 1072/17	Wintrath	KIA on 25/9/17
Albatros D V 2080/17	von Bülow	KIA on 6/1/18
Albatros D V 2086/17	W Papenmeyer	First victory 18/11/17
Albatros D V 2098/17	Reichenbach	Crashed 8/10/17 – black fuselage, white spots
Albatros D V 2346/17	W Papenmeyer	Flown 11/17
Albatros D V 4409/17	Bäumer	Victories 9/9/17 and 20/9/17 – edelweiss
Albatros D V 4430/17	Bäumer	10th-12th and 15th victories 11/17
Albatros D Va 5235/17	W Papenmeyer	Flown 10/12/17 to 12/12/17
Albatros D Va 5373/17*	W Papenmeyer	12/17 to 1/18
Albatros D Va 5375/17*	W Papenmeyer	2nd Victory 4/1/18
Albatros D Va 5395/17	W Papenmeyer	Flown 22/3/18
Albatros D Va 5398/17	W Papenmeyer	
Albatros D Va 5654/17	W Papenmeyer	Flown 10/1/17
Halberstadt CL II 6382/17		Two-seater 'hack'
Fokker D V 2730/16		Conversion trainer
Fokker Dr I 157/17		Black/white bands
Fokker Dr I 190/17	Löffler	Yellow band
Fokker Dr I 195/17	Vallendor	White *V* insignia
Fokker Dr I 203/17	Plange	Additional Iron Cross
Fokker Dr I 204/17	Bäumer	Red-white-black band
Fokker Dr I 212/17	Gallwitz	
Fokker Dr I 213/17	Kempf	
Fokker Dr I 214/17	W Papenmeyer	Destroyed 13/3/18
Fokker Dr I 409/17	W Papenmeyer	KIA 28/3/18
Fokker Dr I 413/17	Bolle	Black-white-yellow bands
Fokker Dr I 493/17	Kempf	4th victory 8/5/18
Fokker D VII 332/18	Löffler	Zigzag lightning bolt
Fokker D VII 4453/18	Lindenberger	OAW-built machine
Fokker D VII F 5109/18		BMW engine

* Confusion exists between these two D Va machines. Papenmeyer's flight log lists D Va 5373/17, while his combat report of 4/1/18 lists D Va 5375/17

COLOUR PLATES

All of the artwork in this section was created by Harry Dempsey, who worked patiently with the author to illustrate the colour schemes as accurately as circumstances will permit. The colours and markings portrayed are approximations at best, and any errors are the author's responsibility. The author owes a great debt to the research of such respected authorities as Alex Imrie, Manfred Thiemeyer, Bruno Schmäling, Ray Rimell and Dave Roberts. The valuable assistance of Dan-San Abbott, Rick Duiven, Dr G K Merrill, Terry Phillips and Dieter Gröschel MD is also appreciated.

1

Albatros D I 431/16 of Ltn Jürgen Sandel, *Jasta* 2, Lagnicourt, October 1916
Sandel's D I was marked with a black *S* on the fuselage in the style typical of the *Staffel* in this early period. The plywood covering of the fuselage appears quite dark, and it may have been stained reddish-brown, but was more likely simply a darker shade of natural-varnished plywood. The wings and tailplane were camouflaged in tones of dark olive green, a light Brunswick green and Chestnut Brown (Venetian Red). Undersides of these surfaces were light blue. The rudder is provisionally shown as painted in in dark green camouflage.

2

Albatros D I (serial unconfirmed) of Ltn d R Diether Collin, *Jasta* 2, Lagnicourt, December 1916
This D I was a very early pre-production machine, possibly 384/16. It had an expansion tank fitted in front of the engine, instead of the more typical triangular tank on top of the engine. It seems to have been painted light green on all uppersurfaces, and was identified by Collin's *Co* emblem in white, with black edging. Prince Friedrich Karl of Prussia later flew this Albatros, and he eventually had the *Co* emblem overpainted with his 'Death's Head' insignia.

3

Albatros D I 390/16 of Ltn d R Otto Walter Höhne, *Jasta* 2, Lagnicourt, September 1916
This machine was marked with *Hö* on the fuselage in black letters, and had reddish-brown camouflage swirls applied to the clear-doped rudder. The wings were camouflaged in the green and brown shades previously described, with light blue undersurfaces. Brushed blotches of reddish-brown stain or paint were randomly applied to the rudder and perhaps the wings as well – a common practice of additional camouflage in *Jasta* 2.

4

Albatros D I 391/16 of Ltn Karl Heinrich Otto Büttner, *Jasta* 2, Lagnicourt, November 1916
This is one of the most famous of early *Jasta* 2 machines but questions still exist concerning its finish. A single dark colour seems to have been applied to the fuselage, interpreted here as a dark brown – however, two or more camouflage shades are also possible. The spinner and nose band were left in light gray. The uppersurfaces of the wings and tailplane were camouflaged in the usual two or three shades described previously. The factory-applied square white cross fields were reduced as evident, and the rudder displayed considerable brushed blotches of stain and a degraded finish.

5

Albatros D II 386/16 of Hptm Oswald Boelcke, *Jasta* 2, Lagnicourt, October 1916
Boelcke apparently applied no distinctive insignia to his D II, other than the wing streamers in the German tricolour. The fuselage was varnished plywood, and there was dense swirled camouflage on the rudder. The uppersurfaces of the wings and tailplane displayed the usual two- or three-colour camouflage. Some random swirl splotches were also seen on the lower left wing at least. This D II had a signal pistol tube protruding from the left side of the cockpit, just below the rim. Boelcke may have achieved his last 14 victories in this aircraft, and died in it on 28 October 1916.

6

Albatros D II 481/16(?) of Ltn Manfred von Richthofen, *Jasta* 2, Lagnicourt, November 1916
Depending on what source is accepted, von Richthofen flew either 481/16 or 491/16. However, there is no guarantee that this aircraft displayed either of those serial numbers. Von Richthofen appears with it in two photographs, and it was marked with a white stripe around the nose. The spinner was either an off-white or very light grey. The rest of this machine likely bore standard factory colours.

7

Albatros D III 2219/16 of Ltn Gerhard Bassenge, *Jasta* 'Boelcke', Proville, July 1917
By the late Spring of 1917, *Jasta* 'Boelcke' had adopted a unit marking of an all white tail unit trimmed in black, as displayed on this D III. Quite often the propeller spinner was black as well. Bassenge's personal markings were the white-bordered black bands on the fuselage. Note that the narrow lengthwise band was applied to the top deck of the fuselage as well. The wings displayed the three-tone camouflage colours of dark and light green and reddish-brown on the uppersurfaces.

8

Albatros D III (serial unknown) of Ltn d R Wilhelm Prien, *Jasta* 'Boelcke', Proville, July 1917
This aircraft is believed to have been formerly flown by 'Fritz' Kempf. He originally applied a lengthwise white 'arrow' marking on the dark fuselage, pointed at both ends. When Prien took it over, he added the white discs connected by a thin white stripe, which extended to the top of the fuselage. The colour of the fuselage is depicted as a dark charcoal grey or faded black, but other colours are plausible alternatives – perhaps even red.

9

Albatros D III (serial unknown) of Ltn Franz Pernet, *Jasta* 'Boelcke', Proville, July 1917
Pernet was photographed in this machine, which

displayed personal markings of three coloured bands edged in white. These have been provisionally interpreted as black/white/black. The usual *Staffel* emblem of a white tail trimmed in black was applied.

10

Albatros D III 796/17 of Ltn d R Georg Noth, *Jasta* 'Boelcke', Proville, May 1917
Noth was shot down by Lt Fry of No 60 Sqn on 19 May 1917. Both Fry's combat report and the description of the captured aircraft (G 39) by RFC technical staff described the fuselage as green with yellow spots. Unfortunately, the available photographs do not permit precise definition of the nose, so the green section is provisionally illustrated as ending at the cockpit. The technical report describes the wings as 'painted green and light blue above and light blue below', but this may have been an error in transcription. The serial number was carefully repainted on the white tail. A large section of the plywood from the starboard side of this D III still exists in Scotland's National Museum of Flight in East Fortune. The yellow spots vary in diameter from 127 mm to 130 mm.

11

Albatros D III 751/17 of Ltn Otto Hunzinger, *Jasta* 'Boelcke', Proville, June 1917
Hunzinger's aeroplane was emblazoned with his initials, artfully worked into the black and white fuselage band. Once again the serial number was displayed on the white tail. Wings were standard three-colour camouflage on the top surfaces and light blue underneath.

12

Albatros D III (serial unknown) of Ltn d R Hermann Frommherz, *Jasta* 'Boelcke', Proville, June 1917
Frommherz called this well-known machine his *'Blaue Maus'* due to its overall light blue finish, which was even applied to the wings. The diagonal black/white sash on the fuselage was an additional personal emblem.

13

Albatros D III (serial unknown) of Ltn d R Werner Voss, *Jasta* 'Boelcke', Proville, May 1917
Werner 'Bubi' Voss displayed his beautifully applied personal emblems of a white-bordered red heart and a white swastika, surrounded by a laurel wreath, on his D III. The spinner is now believed to have been black as per typical *Staffel* practice. Voss took this D III with him to *Jasta* 5 and flew it home to Krefeld in early June. It seems to have had the upper wing eventually replaced, as some photographs show a central radiator, while others show the later offset version. Two white chordwise stripes were painted on the top wing just outboard of the centre section, possibly as leader's markings at *Jasta* 5. Some historians believe that Voss actually had two similarly painted D IIIs.

14

Albatros D V 4409/17 of Uffz Paul Bäumer, *Jasta* 'Boelcke', Varsenaere, September 1917
Bäumer flew this D V for his fifth, sixth and likely seventh victories. His combat report of 20 September describes the white edelweiss painted on a black ground with red stripes. The delineation of the flower emblem is

provisional, as the photograph is a bit vague. Bäumer's use of an edelweiss emblem in both *Jagdstaffeln* 5 and 'Boelcke' led to his nickname of *'Blumen-Heinrich'* (Flower-Henry). This machine displayed the usual *Jasta* markings of a black-trimmed white tail. The wings were probably camouflaged in painted shades of green and mauve on the top surfaces and light blue below.

15

Albatros D V 1072/17 of Ltn d R Johannes Wintrath, *Jasta* 'Boelcke', Varsenaere, September 1917
Notes compiled by historian Dr Gustav Bock from original war diary material contain the information that Wintrath flew D V 1072/17, which was marked with a green-white-green fuselage sash. Two rather mediocre and partial photographs were used for this tentative depiction of the D V Wintrath died in on 25 September 1917. The serial number was marked on the rudder, and the wings were probably painted in green/mauve camouflage. The light 'diamond' shapes on the aft fuselage just ahead of the tail are seen on many D Vs, and are believed to be plywood reinforcements.

16

Albatros D V (pilot and serial unknown), *Jasta* 'Boelcke', Varsenaere, September 1917
This familiar D V was photographed with Bassenge, Kempf and Vallendor. Which one of these pilots generally flew it – if any of them – remains an enigma. The entire fuselage was striped in black and white, and all struts and the undercarriage appear as black. The white tail was uniquely modified by the addition of chordwise black stripes, most likely as supplementary personal insignia. Furthermore, the upper wing bore two white stripes. Interestingly, on 20 October Bassenge flew Albatros D V 2346/17, described as having a 'dark fuselage with black-white bands', but it seems unlikely that this is that machine.

17

Albatros D V 4578/17 of Ltn d R Erwin Böhme, *Jasta* 'Boelcke', Rumbeke, November 1917
Dr Gustav Bock's notes state that Böhme flew this aeroplane at the beginning of November. It displayed a 'natural brown fuselage, green band and on both sides of the fuselage a white B'. The only available photograph shows five-colour printed camouflage fabric on the rudder, and likely wings and tailplane as well. Oddly, when photographed, this D V did not display the usual white tail *Jasta* marking, although this well may have been added later.

18

Albatros D V (serial unknown) of Ltn d R Karl Gallwitz, *Jasta* 'Boelcke', Bavichove, Winter 1917/18
At least one source indicates that this aircraft was Gallwitz' machine, but this is still a very provisional depiction. The fuselage bore a very densely mottled camouflage applied to the uppersurfaces, perhaps with a sponge or rag. This is seen on a few other Albatros fighters of the unit. A coloured band with a dark edging was wrapped around the fuselage, and the wings were covered in five-colour fabric. The tail surfaces displayed the new unit emblem introduced around the beginning of 1918 – half black/half white tail section, with a black border. These colours were

also displayed on the spinner. On 9 October 1917, Gallwitz was recorded as flying D V4407/17 with a 'black fuselage and green band', hence the depiction of the band on this D V as a light green.

19

Albatros D V 4430/17 of Vzfw Paul Bäumer, *Jasta* 'Boelcke', Bavichove, Winter 1917/18

On 7 November 1917 Bäumer scored his tenth victory in D V 4430/17, which was described as having a 'dark fuselage, underneath yellow with white-red-white band', and this is probably that aircraft. It was photographed during Bäumer's visit to his old friends at *Jasta* 5, and by that time it had been painted with the new black/white unit markings on the tail and nose. The photograph indicates a dark mottled camouflage was applied to the upper deck of the fuselage, but the remainder of the plywood covering retained its warm yellow natural varnished finish. Three dark-light-dark diagonal bands are just visible, hence the identification of this D V as 4430/17 – the wings were covered with standard five-colour printed camouflage fabric.

20

Albatros D Va 5373/17 of Ltn d R Wilhelm Papenmeyer, *Jasta* 'Boelcke', January 1918

Papenmeyer achieved his second victory in this D Va on 4 January. His combat report describes the 'yellow' plywood fuselage and black *P* on a white band. At the time the photographs were taken, it had been painted with the black and white *Jasta* markings on spinner and tail. The wings displayed a mixture of painted green/mauve camouflage and five-colour printed fabric.

21

Fokker Dr I 190/17 of Ltn d R Otto Löffler, *Jasta* 'Boelcke', Marcke, February 1918

Löffler's choice of lemon yellow as his personal marking stemmed from the unit colour of his grenadier regiment. The yellow fuselage band was bordered in white, and this Dr I displayed typical black and white *Jasta* markings on the cowling and tail surfaces. The rest of the aircraft bore the usual Fokker streaky camouflage finish on uppersurfaces.

22

Fokker Dr I 203/17 of Ltn d R Richard Plange, *Jasta* 'Boelcke', Marcke, February 1918

Plange's Dr I displayed supplementary Iron Crosses on a light-colored band immediately ahead of the usual national insignia. This has been interpreted here as simply a translucent, dirty or thinly applied white, but the band may well have been light blue or some other very pale colour. Note that the insignia was repeated on top of the fuselage. The aircraft otherwise bore standard unit and factory colours.

23

Fokker Dr I 214/17 of Ltn d R Wilhelm Papenmeyer, *Jasta* 'Boelcke', Marcke, February 1918

Papenmeyer's combat report for his third victory described the personal marking of a black-white-red fuselage band on his Dr I. Close inspection of the photograph reveals a lighter rectangle on the black section of the tailplane, indicating that this machine may once have displayed national insignia on that surface like Bäumer's Dr I 204/17.

24

Fokker Dr I 204/17 of Vzfw Paul Bäumer, *Jasta* 'Boelcke', Marcke, March 1918

Bäumer's triplane was highly decorated, as recorded by his combat report of 9 March 1918. His personal insignia was in the German national black-white-red colours. The tailplane was marked with an additional Iron Cross emblem for the reasons mentioned in the text, and additional insignia were marked on the uppersurface of the bottom wing as well. The rudder was bordered in black, and when photographed, the cross on the port side had been partially outlined.

25

Fokker Dr I 195/17 of Ltn d R Hermann Vallendor, *Jasta* 'Boelcke', Marcke, February/March 1918

Vallendor made sure everyone could identify his aircraft by having large white *V* markings applied to the fuselage and centre section of the top wing. Like 204/17, this aircraft was fitted with two auxiliary struts on the undercarriage wing. This Dr I survived until April/May, and eventually displayed *Balkenkreuze*.

26

Fokker Dr I 209/17 of Vzfw Paul Bäumer, *Jasta* 'Boelcke', Marcke, March 1918

Although he generally flew 204/17, Bäumer certainly seems to have had this reserve aircraft at his disposal. It was marked with a coloured 'B' on the fuselage sides and top. The colour of this emblem is not recorded. The red depicted is one plausible option, as is yellow. When photographed, this Dr I did not show the usual white faceplate on the cowling, which may have been entirely black or possibly factory finish dark olive.

27

Fokker Dr I 494/17(?) of Ltn d R Fritz Kempf, *Jasta* 'Boelcke', Halluin-Ost, April 1918

Kempf's familiar earlier Dr I 213/17 has become almost a cliché among enthusiasts and artists. This later triplane is less well known, but it still featured Kempf's name in large black-outlined characters on the top wing and his famous *KENNSCHT MI NOCH?* legend on the middle wing. The colour of the black-outlined *K* on the fuselage is not confirmed, but yellow is a logical choice. Similarly, the serial number cannot be read on any photograph but was probably 494/17 – the Dr I Kempf flew for his fourth kill.

28

Fokker Dr I 413/17 of Ltn Carl Bolle, *Jasta* 'Boelcke', Halluin-Ost, May 1918

Bolle's Dr I was distinctly marked with the yellow colour of his cuirassier regiment flanked by Prussian black and white stripes. The crosses on the fuselage and rudder have been altered to the later, narrower style of *Balkenkreuze*. A greenish 'wash' was used to modify the white cross backgrounds on the fuselage and wings.

29

Fokker Dr I 157/17 (pilot unknown), *Jasta* 'Boelcke', Halluin-Ost, May 1918

The regular pilot of this Dr I remains unidentified. When photographed in an earlier guise with Iron Cross insignia, this aircraft was individually identified simply by the five black(?) and white vertical stripes on the fuselage. By the time it displayed the form of *Balkenkreuz* insignia seen in the profile – in May 1918 – the black and white stripe décor had been extended to the interplane struts.

30

Fokker Dr I (serial unknown) of Ltn d R Hermann Frommherz, *Jasta* 'Boelcke', Halluin-Ost, May 1918
Frommherz was photographed posing with this Dr I, and he is thought to have flown it after he returned to the *Staffel* in May 1918. The personal identification consisted of a black(?) and white 'diamond' band around the fuselage, and this was repeated as sawtooth markings on the struts. When Frommherz posed with this machine, the cowling did not show the usual white faceplate seen on most triplanes of the unit. Note the black-outlined rudder on this and the previous machine.

31

Fokker Dr I 204/17 of Vzfw Paul Bäumer, *Jasta* 'Boelcke', Halluin-Ost, April 1918
This Dr I went through considerable alterations in markings during its existence. By April the national insignia had been converted to the initial 'thick' form of *Balkenkreuze,* with a low ratio of length to width. In addition the tips of all three wings were painted black, generally with very narrow white-red borders on the inboard edge. The Iron Cross emblems on the lower wings were overpainted with camouflage colour, but that on the tailplane was also converted to a *Balkenkreuz.*

32

Fokker D VII 332/18 of Ltn d R Otto Löffler, *Jasta* 'Boelcke', Mont Soissons Ferme, circa July 1918
Early production D VIIs displayed the familiar Fokker streaky camouflage finish on their fuselages. 332/18 was one of a small batch that had their serial numbers stencilled in white on the fuselage. The *Jasta* colours were painted on the tailplane and aft fuselage, and the white nose was a further *Staffel* identification. The personal insignia consisted of a white zigzag lightning bolt with a thin black edging applied to the sides and top of the fuselage. The association of this machine with Löffler is provisional, based on some notes discovered in the A E Ferko archives held by the University of Texas, in Dallas.

33

Fokker D VII (pilot and serial unknown), *Jasta* 'Boelcke', Emerchicourt, September 1918
The details of this Fokker-built D VII are lost, but it was marked by a nicely executed ace of spades on a black(?) bordered white band. Both sides of the fin were painted white on all *Jasta* 'Boelcke' D VIIs. This Fokker otherwise bore typical *Staffel* markings and four-colour printed camouflage fabric.

34

Fokker D VII (OAW) 4453/18 of Ltn Alfred Lindenberger, *Jasta* 'Boelcke', Aniche, November 1918
The depiction of Lindenberger's striped OAW-built D VII in yellow and black is entirely provisional, based on his award of Württemberg's Gold Military Merit Medal. This D VII had four-colour fabric on the wings and the usual

Staffel markings on nose and tail. By the time it was photographed at Nivelles in the postwar period its colours were quite degraded.

35

Fokker D VII (pilot and serial unknown), *Jasta* 'Boelcke', Aniche, November 1918
This Fokker-built D VII was photographed in RAF hands after the war. The unknown pilot's individual insignia consisted of the white *K* on a black(?) fuselage band, and a nicely delineated white arrow with black edging. The aircraft was covered in four-colour fabric. Some may be tempted to associate this D VII with 'Fritz' Kempf, but he had left the *Jasta* on 18 August. This D VII was photographed at least three months later, but it is slightly possible that some other pilot had continued to fly Kempf's old D VII without changing the insignia.

36

Fokker D VII (F) of Oblt Carl Bolle, *Jasta* 'Boelcke', Aniche, November 1918
Bolle flew *at least* two separate D VIIs in the course of the war, but this is the BMW-engined machine that was turned in at Nivelles after the armistice. It boasted his usual black, white and yellow personal bands on the fuselage. The rest of the fuselage appears to have been painted black, with the exception of the unit markings. The upper wing bore two white chordwise stripes on the centre section, the rest of which was covered in four-colour fabric.

ACKNOWLEDGEMENTS

First and foremost, the author owes an incalculable debt to his friend and esteemed historian Norman Franks, whose wonderful book *Jasta Boelcke - The History of Jasta 2 1916-1918* was the inspiration and extremely valuable source for the present work. Norman's depth of research, scholarship and generosity are amazing, and anyone wishing to know more of this unit should acquire a copy of his book. The assistance and research of Alex Imrie and Manfred Thiemeyer is greatly appreciated. As always, grateful thanks go to Rick Duiven and Dieter H M Gröschel MD for sharing valuable information from their scholarly studies. A series of translations of Böhme's letters by Doug Fant (edited by Marvin Skelton), together with the research of Dr-Ing Niedermeyer, resulted in a number of superb articles in *Over the Front* which were of tremendous value. Adam Wait, Peter Kilduff and O'Brien Browne also provided indispensable translations of German material. The staff members of the History of Aviation Collection in the University of Texas in Dallas were helpful as always. Thanks are extended to Terry 'Taz' Phillips, Reinhard Zankl and Lance Bronnenkant for photographs. Dan-San Abbott, Jörn Leckscheid, Stephen Lawson, Jon Guttman, Ray Rimell, Reinhard Kastner and too many others to name all gave unselfishly of their time and material. The author's many colleagues at *Over the Front* (www.overthefront.com), *Cross and Cockade International* (www.crossandcockade.com), and *The Aerodrome Forum* (www.theaerodrome.com) were helpful as usual, and their web sites are highly recommended.

BIBLIOGRAPHY

BOELCKE, O, *Hauptmann Bölckes Feldberichte*, Gotha, 1917

BOELCKE, O, *An Aviator's Field Book*, Nashville, 1991

BÖHME, E, (WERNER, J, ED.), *Briefe eines deutschen Kampffliegers an ein junges Mädchen*, Leipzig, 1930

BOLLE, RITTM. A.D. CARL, 'Jagdstaffel Boelcke (30.August 1916 – 24.November 1918)', in anthology *In der Luft Unbesiegt*, Georg Paul Neumann, ed., Munich, 1923

BOLLE, RITTM. A.D. CARL, 'Jagdstaffel Boelcke', in anthology *Unsere Luftstreitkräfte*, Walter von Eberhardt, ed., Berlin, 1930

BRONNENKANT, L, PhD, *The Imperial German Eagles in World War I*, Atglen, 2006

DIGGENS, B, *September Evening*, London, 2003

FERKO, A E, *Richthofen*, Berkhamsted, 1995

FRANKS, N, BAILEY, F, AND GUEST, R, *Above the Lines*, London, 1993

FRANKS, N, GUEST, G, AND BAILEY, F, *Bloody April - Black September*, London 1995

FRANKS, N, *Jasta Boelcke*, London, 2004

FRANKS, N, BAILEY, F AND DUIVEN, R, *The Jasta Pilots*, London, 1996

FRANKS, N, BAILEY, F AND DUIVEN, R, *The Jasta War Chronology*, London, 1998

FRANKS, N, GIBLIN, H, *Under the Guns of the Kaiser's Aces*, London, 2003

FRANKS, N, GIBLIN, H, *Under the Guns of the German Aces*, London, 1997

FRY, W M, *Air of Battle*, London, 1974

GOOTE, T, *In Trichtern und Wolken*, Berlin, 1934

GROSZ, P M, 'The Agile and Aggressive Albatros', *Air Enthusiast No 1*, 1976

GROSZ, P M, *Albatros D I/D II Windsock Datafile 100*, Berkhamsted, 2003

GROSZ, P M, *Albatros D III, Windsock Datafile Special*, Berkhamsted, 2003

HALLER, H, *Der Flieger von Rottenburg*, Bayreuth, 1939

HENSHAW, T, *The Sky Their Battlefield*, London 1995

IMRIE, A, *Osprey Airwar 13 – German Fighter Units 1914-May 1917*, London, 1978

IMRIE, A, *Osprey Airwar 17 – German Fighter Units June 1917-1918*, London, 1978

IMRIE, A, 'Paul Bäumer – Iron Eagle', *Cross & Cockade Journal*, Vol 5 No 4, 1964

IMRIE, A, *Pictorial History of the German Army Air Service*, London, 1971

IMRIE, A, *The Fokker Triplane*, London, 1992

IMRIE, A, *Vintage Warbirds 16 - German Army Air Aces of World War One*, Poole, 1987

JENTSCH, K F K, *Jagdflieger im Feuer*, Magdeburg, 1937

KILDUFF, P, *Richthofen - Beyond the Legend of the Red Baron*, New York, 1993

KILDUFF, P, *The Illustrated Red Baron*, London, 1999

LÜBKE, A, *Oswald Boelcke der Meisterflieger*, Reutlingen, 1941

NIEDERMEYER, DR-ING, 'A Retrospective View of Ltn. Erwin Böhme', *Over the Front*, Various Issues 1990-2002, with translations by Fant, D, edited by Skelton, M

O'CONNOR, N, *Aviation Awards of Imperial Germany in World War I and the Men Who Earned Them,* Vols I to VII, Princeton NJ and Atglen PA, 1988 to 2003

PUGLISI, W R AND MILLER, T G, 'Jasta B', *Cross & Cockade Journal*, Vol 9, No 4, 1968

REVELL, A, *British Single-Seater Fighter Squadrons on the Western Front in World War I*, Atglen, 2006

REVELL, A, *High in the Empty Blue*, Mountain View, 1995

RICHTHOFEN, M VON, *Der rote Kampfflieger*, Berlin, 1933

RIMELL, R, *Albatros Fighters Special*, Berkhamsted, 1991

RIMELL, R (ED), *Fokker D VII Anthology No 1*, Berkhamsted, 1997

SCHILLING, F, *Flieger an allen Fronten*, Berlin, 1936

SCHMÄLING, B, 'Ltn Paul Bäumer and his Fokker Dr I 204/17', *Cross & Cockade Journal*, Vol 23 No 4, 1982

TUTSCHEK, A, *Stürme und Liftsiege*, Berlin, 1918

TUTSCHEK, A, 'The War Letters of Hauptmann Adolf Ritter von Tutschek' *Over the Front*, Vol 3 No 4, Vol 4 No 1, 1988-89

WERNER, J, *Boelcke; der Mensch, der Flieger, der Führer der deutschen Jagdfliegerei*, Leipzig, 1932

ZUERL, W, *Pour le Mérite-Flieger*, Munich, 1938

INDEX

References to illustrations are shown in **bold**. Plates are shown with page and caption locators in brackets.